D0503086

Solo Schooling

Learn to Coach Yourself
when You're Riding on Your Own

Wendy Jago

Northern Plains Public Library
Ault Colorado

J.A. ALLEN · LONDON

© Wendy Jago 2003
First published in Great Britain 2003
Reprinted 2003

ISBN 0 85131 859 2

J.A. Allen
Clerkenwell House
Clerkenwell Green
London EC1R OHT

J.A. Allen is an imprint of Robert Hale Ltd

The right of Wendy Jago to be identified as author
of this work has been asserted by her in accordance
with the Copyright, Design and Patents Act 1988

British Library Cataloguing in Publication Data
A catalogue record for this book is available from the British Library

Photographs by Leo Jago, except for the following, which are produced by permission:
those on pages 8, 21 by permission of Andrea Moffat; on page 203 (and lower left jacket
photograph) by permission of Kevin Sparrow; on pages 145, 173, 208 by permission of
Image Point Event Photography

Line illustrations on pages 61 and 62 by Rodney Paull, from author's sketches

Edited by Martin Diggle
Design by Paul Saunders
Colour Separation by Tenon & Polert Colour Scanning Ltd.
Printed in China by Midas Printing International Ltd.

Dedication

For solo schoolers everywhere
through fair weather and foul
I'm with you all the way.

Contents

Acknowledgements   x
Introduction   1

PART ONE   *The Distinctiveness of an NLP Coaching Approach*   5

1   *Why Take a Coaching Approach to Riding?*   6
How Coaching Developed   7
Coaching and NLP   9
Core Features of an NLP Coaching Approach   11

2   *Taking a Coaching Approach – The Basic Assumptions*   23
Truth, Assumptions and Presuppositions   23
Enabling Presuppositions   24

PART TWO   *Getting Started*   39

3   *Becoming More Aware*   40
Developing Sensory Acuity   41
Calibration – Spotting Differences and Changes   45
Skill-building Tips   48

4   *Triangulation*   50
How Triangulation Works   52
Sensory System Check   55
Logical Level Check   56
Summarizing the Process   58

Triangulation in Action – Working with Nikki G   59

5 *Designing Your Motivation* 65
Preferred Chunk Size 67
Direction of Motivation 71
Method of Approach 74
Source of Reference 78
Orientation in Time 82
Plotting Your Meta-programmes 86

Meta-programmes in Action – Working with Nicky M 90

6 *Motivating Your Horse* 95
Profiling Your Horse's Meta-programmes 97

Meta-programmes in Action II – Working with Georgie Boy 107

7 *The Importance of Framing* 110
The Curiosity Frame 112
The Success/Failure Frame 113
Moving from a Success/Failure Frame into a Curiosity Frame 115
The 'As-if' Frame 116
Opening up Resourcefulness 120

Framing in Action – Working with Jo and Nikki G 120

8 *Getting it Into Words* 124
Your Language and Your Coding 125
Language, States and Behaviour 127
Change the Language, Change the Experience 131
Weasel Words 132

Words in Action – Wendy and Nikki G 139

PART THREE *Groundwork* 143

9 *Getting What You Really Want* 144
What do You Really, Really Want? 147
Well-formed Goals 151
Keeping on Track (Chunking Up and Down) 152
Owning Your Riding 155

Goals in Action – Sean and Kluedo 156

10 *Traps and States* 158
Traps 158
States 166

Playtime – Wendy and Nikki G 172

PART FOUR *Coaching in Action* 175

11 *Coaching Yourself with Questions* 176
Leading Questions 176

12 *Structuring the Work Session* 181
Stage One: Warm-up 183
Stage Two: Workout 184
Stage Three: Cool-down 185

Structure in Action – Sean and Harry 187

PART FIVE *Developing Magnificence* 193

Nikki G 195
Nicky M 199
Sean 204
Marisian – the Ultimate Solo Schooler 208

Conclusion 216

Appendix – Sub-modalities 218
Taking Things Further 221
Index 223

Acknowledgements

Writing this book has been a delightful experience, to a large extent because of all those who have contributed their enthusiasm, encouragement and expertise at every stage. The following have a special place in this book and in my heart.

Caroline Burt, my publisher; Martin Diggle, my editor; and Paul Saunders my designer, who all nurtured my idea and made it come alive so splendidly.

Sean Burgess, Nikki Green and Nicky Moffatt, for their willingness to become involved with a different kind of learning experience and to explore every stage with me both on and off horse.

Marisian Pritchard, for sharing her ideas over the years and for exemplifying the thoughtful, passionate and playful art of solo schooling so naturally and splendidly.

Charles de Kunffy, Karen Broxton, Alex Drew and Debby Lush, whose generously shared expertise and reflections inspired and honed my own. While I owe many insights and ideas to them, my limitations are entirely my mine.

My husband, Leo, who is so often the hand for my words when I judge, and who, through his photographs, has also become the lens for my eye. His encouragement and support and that of our daughter, Charlotte, is unfailing and unstinting.

Jan Elfline and Ian McDermott, who showed me the special qualities of coaching.

Finally, the horses – especially Georgie, Kluedo, Beamish, Lucinda and Lolly. Any proof that we needed of the value of this way of working has been provided both by their readiness to play and by the development of their inherent magnificence.

Introduction

BECAUSE A NUMBER of the ideas presented in this book may be new to many people, I thought it would be useful to provide a brief synopsis of the essential ideas discussed in each chapter. I hope that this will encourage you to embrace the exciting opportunities available to the solo schooler.

Part One – The Distinctiveness of an NLP Coaching Approach

Chapter 1. Why Take a Coaching Approach to Riding?
How coaching differs from teaching, and what it has to offer you. The roots of coaching. Excellence and effectiveness – NLP and the Inner Game. The core assumptions of the coaching approach.

Chapter 2. Taking a Coaching Approach – The Basic Assumptions
What do we need to know about the process of coaching ourselves? The building blocks of working with ourselves as solo schoolers.

Part Two – Getting Started

Chapter 3. Becoming More Aware
Developing your skills as an observer – of yourself and your horse. What

exactly is going on? How is it different if you take a different perceptual position? How do you know what to look out for? Calibrating changes.

Chapter 4. Triangulation
The key to knowing where you are and moving on. Putting yourself on the map. Where are you now? Where are you going? How do you know what progress you're making?

Triangulation in Action: Nikki G

Chapter 5. Designing Your Motivation
What gets you going? Meta-programmes (major behavioural patterns) explained. Recognizing, using and developing your meta-programme skills. Profiling your patterns so you can coach yourself better. Key programmes for solo schoolers.

Meta-programmes in Action: Nicky M

Chapter 6. Motivating Your Horse
Owners and riders have always been able to describe their horse's nature and how he responds to things. In other words, they recognize that he has characteristic patterns of response and behaviour. I propose the idea that horses have meta-programmes too. How to build a meta-programme profile of your horse, so that you can talk to him in his language and dovetail your training programme to fit in with his individual profile.

Meta-programmes in Action: Georgie Boy

Chapter 7. The Importance of Framing
What framing is, and why it is important. The effects of framing things in different ways; choosing the best frame for the job in hand. The curiosity frame; the success/failure frame; the 'as-if' frame. Opening up resourcefulness; turning feedback into feed-forward.
Framing in Action: Jo and Nikki G

Chapter 8. Getting it into Words
Words and body-language. Language that blocks you and language that helps you. Language and internal representation. Becoming your own interpreter. Finding the words that work for you – and training yourself and others to use them!

Words in Action: Wendy and Nikki G

Part Three – Groundwork

Chapter 9. Getting What You Really Want

Well-formed outcomes. Using the roles of Dreamer, Realist and Critic (the core components of the NLP Disney Creativity Strategy) in their proper places to help you form and achieve your goals. Chunking. Holding your agenda. Accountability. Training your trainer.

Goals in Action: Sean and Kluedo

Chapter 10. Traps and States

What are the traps that lure you as a solo schooler? Recognition and avoidance. Disabling self-destruct sequences.

The concept of REPLAY:

R ecognizing, managing and designing states

E xploring your most effective schooling state

P leasure

L earning

A ctivity

Y es-set.

Playtime

Part Four – Coaching in Action

Chapter 11. Coaching Yourself With Questions

Asking powerful questions. Questioning yourself. Questioning your horse.

Chapter 12. Structuring the Work Session

The seamless stages of a working session

1. Warm-up
   tuning-in
   freeing and unblocking
   framing

2. Workout
   exploring
   resourcing
   focusing and forwarding the action

3. Cool-down
　unwinding
　celebrating
　marking the learning
　thinking forward.

Structure in Action: Sean and Harry

Part Five – Case-studies of Developing Magnificence

Nikki G – posture, stretch and independence
Nicky M – from pulling out to opting in
Sean – getting his head around being excellent
Marisian – the ultimate solo schooler

PART 1

The Distinctiveness of an NLP Coaching Approach

1

Why Take a Coaching Approach to Riding?

IF YOU REGULARLY RIDE ON YOUR OWN, either between riding lessons or because you don't currently have a riding teacher, this book will help you make your riding more purposeful, more enjoyable and more effective. It will show you how to develop some straightforward but powerful skills which enable you to get the most from yourself and your horse.

Being a coach is not the same as being a teacher, and being your own coach – either in between lessons or without lessons – is not the same as being your own teacher. Teachers need a body of expertise in their subject, and usually their expertise is in advance of their pupil's: coaches understand what's involved in learning and change, and how to help you find the resources you need to achieve what you really want. Because coaching is concerned with *process* not *content;* with *how* things happen rather than *what* happens, a coach can give invaluable help even in a field they know little about. This works because the person being coached already has much of the information that's necessary; the coaching will help them sort out what else they may need.

This approach can be applied to riding. A coach, whether face-to-face with you or from within the pages of this book, will be asking you questions that help you to go inside yourself – and inside your relationship with your horse – to search for answers. You are likely to be surprised by how much you know: about what's going wrong, about what changes need to be made, and about how you can go about making them. That's the miraculous aspect of coaching – it leaves you feeling more powerful, more knowledgeable and more resourceful, but without telling you what to do or how to do it. The agenda is yours.

This book will coach you, and it will go beyond that to show you how you can become your own coach. If you are a relative newcomer to riding, it will help you recognize when you need to find more options or ask for more technical help, and it will also help you to grow in confidence alongside the teaching you have, rather than becoming over-dependent on your teacher. If you are already more experienced, it will help you to refine and develop your skills, and it will give you ways to help yourself out of stuck places, pitfalls, puzzlement and despondency. And, whether you are a newcomer or an experienced rider, the benefits you receive will be passed on to your horse in terms of achievable goals, clearer messages and less of the emotional clutter which forms a kind of 'white noise' that confuses and distracts him from what you're really trying to communicate.

How Coaching Developed

Coaching has grown into a modern profession over the last thirty years, with a huge increase during the 1990s. While there have been sports coaches for much longer than this, their approach was often one of 'teach and tell', encouraging pupils or those being coached to meet training targets and prepare for competitions. In the 1970s, a tennis coach named Timothy Gallwey discovered a new approach that seemed to be more effective than this: he found that the less he commented, the less he judged his pupils in terms of right and wrong. And the more he encouraged them to develop a state of 'relaxed focus' on what they were doing, how they were doing it and what resulted, the more they progressed. Gallwey set down his findings in the form of an equation:

$$Performance = Potential - Interference$$

In other words, what you achieve is directly proportional to how *little* you – or anyone else – interfere(s) with your own potential. And in his famous *Inner Game* books (*Tennis, Golf, Skiing, Music* and, most recently, *Work*) Gallwey pointed the finger at two frequent sources of interference.

One was the part of ourselves which tells us what we ought to be doing and not doing, makes judgements based on success and failure and continuously tells us we should be trying harder. Gallwey called this Self One, and pointed out that this conscious part of the mind doesn't really have the ability to monitor and control physical coordination and skill development anyway. (If you have ever injured your dominant hand and had to 'explain' to the other hand how to do something really simple, like cleaning your teeth, you will appreciate this point.) Instead, coordination is organized by the unconscious, inner part of the mind, which Gallwey called Self Two. In his view, Self One often undermines our trust in our instinctive, natural processing, and gets in the way of progress and achievement in any area of learning or skill that involves it. If you are consciously 'trying' to apply the correct aids for a canter strike-off, or a half-pass, the result is likely to be tense, wooden and riddled with effort. However, if you know what signals your horse has been taught to respond to and then simply think 'right canter', or 'forward and sideways', your message is likely to be clearer and subtler, and the result more fluent and expressive. This is because your mind and body are interconnected in very subtle ways. If your horse is fully attentive to you, he will sense the slight differences brought about in your body by the change in your thinking. These are the best signals of all – for both of you.

Gallwey's second finding was that, even when trainers praised their pupils, they were setting up or reinforcing a success/failure mind-set in the pupil which, in turn, encouraged Self One (trying) rather than Self Two (doing naturally). Praise is actually part of the same framework as blame: even though it feels better to be praised, we are still left judging ourselves rather than developing our curiosity and awareness. Think of how you felt when you had to repeat something your teacher had praised you for: 'What if I don't do as well this

'Trying' and tense – Nicky and Lucinda. Contrast with the photo on page 21.

time?'; 'Now just how did I get it that good?'; 'Can I live up to her expectations/my reputation?' – these may have been the kinds of thoughts that went through your mind.

Gallwey found that when he got his pupils to focus their attention on what they were actually experiencing and to notice relevant details about it, they not only gained useful information but also developed a state of relaxed concentration which helped them to learn and perform to the best of their ability. By taking away the jabbering of Self One (internal interference) and the judgemental comments of the teacher (external interference), Gallwey helped his pupils to achieve their potential. His role in the process was to focus attention and to ask relevant questions – and, often, even this became minimal as his pupils learnt to do the same for themselves. The attitude of curiosity, and the state of relaxed awareness which curiosity promotes, was the key that helped them achieve their potential, where 'trying' and even encouragement (from themselves or from people they respected) got in the way.

It's this kind of approach which has now spread far beyond the tennis courts and golf ranges where it was first developed. Golfers and tennis players have other roles as workers and managers, with busy lives at home and in their communities. Coaching approaches and skills they learnt in one sphere got applied in others. Gallwey and the other coaches he trained were asked to help with business consultancy and training. Nowadays, this kind of coaching has many practitioners and many applications: life coaching and business coaching are two recent growth areas.

Coaching and NLP

Recently, coaching has been brought together with Neuro-Linguistic Programming (NLP), resulting in a powerful combination of enabling approaches and specific techniques – NLP Coaching. (To find out more about this, see the section on Taking Things Further at the back of this book.)

In my previous book, *Schooling Problems Solved with NLP* (J.A. Allen, 2001), I showed how NLP can help you to understand yourself as a rider and to communicate with your horse more effectively. Riding is a unique sport because it involves working with another living creature, whose understanding of the world is different from ours in many important ways. Therefore it is essential for us to understand not only what messages we want to give him, but also how we can give them clearly and in such a way that he is most likely to understand what we intend. NLP is a body of information about how people go about things: how they behave; how they think; how they interact; how they are effective and ineffective. Because it describes exactly what's involved in thinking and communicating (the nuts and bolts processes that everyone shares, as well as those which are individual to you or me), it offers us really useful skills for making the most of ourselves as riders and communicating more effectively with our horses.

Just as you can think of the function of bits in general, the effect of a specific kind of bit in particular, and the fit and action of a particular bit for a particular horse, doing a certain kind of work in a particular situation, so NLP gives you recipes for thinking and behaviour that seem to fit most people, ways of discovering the patterns that are unique to one individual, and ways of making the most of your own uniqueness in a given situation. Like coaching, NLP is non-judgemental. It describes things without labelling them as 'good' or 'bad', 'success' or 'failure'. Perhaps even more importantly, the huge amount of observation and inquiry on which NLP can now draw to understand and help people shows that labels like these just don't help. Most ways of thinking and behaving are appropriate, or effective, *in some circumstances* – and less so in others. If we become curious without making judgements, we learn more and remain in a better state of mind to apply what we've learnt. This is one of the understandings that NLP and coaching have in common.

While coaching was developed as a way of helping other people, we can also learn to apply it to ourselves. In this book I'm going to concentrate on exploring how you can take a coaching approach when you're working alone, or thinking about riding on your own, and how this can help you to become more effective as a rider. As mentioned previously, coaching skills aren't just confined to riding, or even to sport. They involve a way of looking at ourselves and interacting with ourselves, and so they can rapidly become a habit, spilling over helpfully into other areas of our lives.

If coaching is an approach, NLP often provides specific tools that we can use within that approach. NLP provides us with a kind of 'owner's manual' for our own brains – a way of describing and understanding how they work. (If you'd like a more systematic understanding of NLP and riding, you'll find it in my previous book, *Schooling Problems Solved with NLP*.) Coaching is always ultimately focused on goals, and its aim is to create purpose and effective action. Where a particular NLP concept or technique can be used to help in this way within a coaching approach, I'll explain what it is and how you can apply it.

In the rest of this chapter I'm going to set out briefly the core features of taking the coaching approach to yourself and how it differs from what you may be used to in your riding experience. I'll explain briefly how you can benefit from taking this kind of approach. It's likely that, as you read on, you may at times recognize your own experience, and this can be the start of becoming really curious about how things you may have taken for granted up until now can be helpful or obstructive to you. These key features are the underlying themes that run through this book: the skeleton on which its specific chapters and exercises are built up.

Core Features of an NLP Coaching Approach

Assuming Resourcefulness

Assume resourcefulness in yourself and others (which includes your horse) *as opposed to being critical, undermining, black-and-white, having fixed beliefs or attitudes.*

Do you ever think things like: 'I'm not good enough for my horse'; 'I'll never be able to ride as well as my trainer'; 'He's too old to learn that now'; 'Heavy horses can't do dressage'; 'I'll never manage to get him to stay on the bit'; 'Horses are lazy, that's why he won't go forward'?

All these statements have in-built assumptions which basically involve beliefs about resourcefulness and ability. NLP was founded on extensive and careful observation of outstandingly effective people, and it emerged that believing the best of others tended to bring out the best in them, while

The myth that 'heavy horses can't do dressage' – Sean and Georgie.

thinking of them as limited tended to have exactly the opposite effect. NLP calls these kinds of prior beliefs **presuppositions** – in other words, we go into a situation presupposing how people will behave, what motivates them, and how things will work out. This narrows down what can happen, because what we think and feel gets translated into our actions, whether we intend it or not. The early developers of NLP found that some presuppositions are more useful than others: for example, presupposing that people are resourceful isn't necessarily *true*, but it's no more untrue than presupposing that they are limited, lazy, likely to be hostile or uncooperative. And if you make a positive assumption about someone you'll tend to behave positively and so create the very conditions that help them produce their best. So a presumption of resourcefulness weighs the odds in its favour.

Let's take a couple of examples to illustrate this point:

YOU TRY SOMETHING out with your horse and it doesn't work.

'I'm not good enough to bring that off', you think. You may give it up and try something easier. Or you might grit your teeth and try again ('persevere,' says that little voice in your head), but you're disappointed, despondent, and so you're tense, tentative, and it goes even worse the second time. 'There, I knew I couldn't do it', you think.

What happens if you give yourself the benefit of the doubt? 'I don't seem to be able to get this right – yet', you think. You decide you were a bit ambitious, and plan to ask your teacher's help when next you see her. You're disappointed, but you haven't written yourself off. Or you think carefully about what happened, and decide to give it another go, making a small change in how you approach the manoeuvre. In other words, you refine and experiment. This time, it works better. Not only do you have a good feeling, but also you've learnt something from thinking the problem through and making adjustments.

YOUR HORSE SEEMS sluggish when you take him into the school. 'Got to get him motivated', you think, and give him a thump with your legs. He goes forward all right, but he rushes and seems stiff.

Or perhaps you think, instead, 'He seems a bit dull today. I wonder if it's because of that long hack yesterday (or that collected work we did). Perhaps I should spend longer just loosening him up at his pace before asking him to go forward more. Let's just see what happens.' And after some time of walking and cantering in a large frame he seems to pick up energy and enthusiasm.

Getting into an Appropriate Resourceful State

Get into an appropriate and resourceful state for your riding *as opposed to not recognizing your state or that of others, or being stuck in a state that inhibits or limits you.*

IF YOU HAVE YOUR own horse, or a share of one, you can't always be in the best frame of mind for riding. You may have to ride early in the morning or in the evening to fit around work. Even if you don't work, you may be under pressure or fed up for any number of reasons which have nothing to do with riding. Or you may be upset because the last time you rode he bucked you off, or things just didn't go well, and you're worried that the same may happen this time. All these things will put you in a mind-body state which is less than effective for riding, and which may actually limit what you can do. Perhaps more importantly, the negative, tired or worried state you are experiencing will be communicated through your body to your horse. He can't understand what's going on for you, of course – he will just feel your anxiety or tension. If he's a sensitive soul, he may seem to 'catch' what you're feeling himself. Or he may just become confused.

Horses don't understand human emotion, and we have no way of clarifying it for them. All the professionals I've talked to have quite separately made the point that emotion has to be left outside the schooling arena. That way, you and your horse can pay full and uncontaminated attention to each other's behaviour. It's like having your mind fully on a conversation, as opposed to going through the motions while half of your mind is thinking about something else. When that happens, both you and your conversational partner really know your mind is elsewhere, and the conversation is only half-hearted. If your partner doesn't know what's going on for you, they're likely to feel cheated of the attention they expect. Then they may get irritable, or withdraw emotionally. Horses can react in the same way, and for the same reasons.

So having the ability to recognize, choose and change your states can help your riding a lot. This concept is explored further in Chapter 10.

Defining Clear and Achievable Outcomes

Have clear and achievable outcomes *as opposed to riding without clear outcomes or having outcomes which are unrealistic.*

> YOU GO INTO THE SCHOOL. It's a fine morning and you're looking forward to a nice ride. You walk around a bit to loosen the muscles, then do a little walk, trot and canter. Perhaps a bit of shoulder-in, a rein-back, some lengthened strides. Forty minutes go by. You go back into the yard. 'How did he go?', asks a friend. 'OK, I suppose', you say – but actually you don't really remember what you did or know whether it was good or not. You've been drifting around doing a bit of this and a bit of that. You didn't have an aim, and so you don't have anything to measure the work against.
>
> Or perhaps you have begun to realize that, although your horse is a nice enough chap, he's tending to plod around without much energy. Your partner was hanging over the fence last week and said rudely 'You seem to be working harder than he is!' So you decided that you need to get your horse to go forward more, with less nagging. You asked your teacher what she would recommend and she suggested lots of transitions, both within and between the gaits. So today that's what you're going to work on. You keep this in the forefront of your mind throughout, and by the end of the session your horse does seem to be sharper and more forward. You go in feeling pleased because you've achieved your aim and noticed the beginnings of a difference.

NLP and coaching both emphasize how valuable it is to have clear outcomes, which are realistic and achievable step by step. And, by studying people who did achieve their aims, examining their behaviour and asking them how they thought and felt inside, the NLP developers identified a set of guidelines which will ensure that your desired outcome is 'well-formed' – that is, set up in such a way that it's likely to be achieved. There's more about outcomes in Chapter 9.

Making Choices that Fit You

Make choices that fit with who you are and what you believe *as opposed to just doing what others advise or tell you to.*

> AS AN INEXPERIENCED rider or new horse-owner, it's easy to follow the lead of people with more experience and knowledge. It's hard to resist entering your first competition if your trainer tells you that you're ready and if everyone else at the yard is off competing every weekend. It's hard to say: 'I'm scared he'll run away with me' to a friend who is urging you to 'Come for a lovely blast on the downs',

or 'Please don't put the fence up another notch – it looks too high for me' when your trainer is saying how scopy your horse is and how he won't notice the extra couple of inches.

So you go for the hack, and feel so anxious the whole way that you don't enjoy it. Or perhaps your tension communicates itself to your horse, so that he becomes spooky and wound up. Perhaps you give in and enter the competition – lie awake the night before, feel sick in the morning, forget the test or the plan of the jumping round, wish you'd never agreed... Or you freeze as you approach that raised fence, so your horse stops and you shoot off over his head. These examples all show how important it is to know what you feel and want, and to respect your right to go with that rather than with what others are telling you. It's not usually a question of right and wrong, but rather one involving differences in perception, values or beliefs. Some children love competing, but I knew one who made it quite clear that although she wanted to be able to do everything at home, or with her teacher, she had no interest in doing it in public. Wisely, her proud parents let her decide instead of pushing her. It would have been much easier for them to urge, persuade or compel her – and then perhaps she might have given up altogether. We all need to own our experience and our decisions.

Equally, it's important to think about what more experienced people are telling you, and to be willing to move into your 'stretch zone' if you can. Learning doesn't happen in your comfort zone any more than it does in your panic zone! One sensitive rider I know told me how grateful she is to a rather domineering teacher she had, because when her horse spooked into a sudden canter he told her to ride the canter forward for a circuit or two of the school, rather than immediately trying to stop. 'Now I know I can stay with my horse if he spooks', she told me. 'I can use that energy to get better quality work from him, and I can get him to stop when I want to through correct and subtle signals instead of rough and ready ones. I wouldn't have learnt that if my trainer hadn't pushed me that day.'

The idea of zones is a useful one, and helps us to steer our learning effectively so that we don't get bored with what is too familiar on the one hand, or too frightened by what is new on the other. As the American psychologist Abraham Maslow pointed out in the 1960s, human beings need safety and they need growth. Too much safety tends to become boring and propel us in the direction of new experience – growth; and too much growth can be scary and propel us in the direction of safety again. In particular, the idea of a midway stretch zone where new learning is both demanding and manageable is a help-ful guide. We need to respect both advice from others and our own gut feelings. This way, we can work out whether something is too much to ask of ourselves just now, or whether it may be a useful and achievable stretch.

As the last example showed, it doesn't do us good to stay forever within our comfort zone, any more than it does to let ourselves be pushed into the panic zone. There is no learning, no progress, in either. When you take on the responsibility of a coaching approach to yourself, looking at what these zones mean for you, and finding out more about the stretch zone which lies between, is an important part of your responsibility to yourself.

Permitting Yourself to Play

Give yourself and your horse permission to play, to be wrong, to experi-ment, to recap, to retreat, to change direction *as opposed to 'trying' all the time, being hard on 'failures', playing safe, or slogging on regardless.*

Most of us took up riding 'for fun'. Once we become committed to it, and to our horses, the fun sometimes disappears, and things like effort take its place. In my experience it's a mistake to confuse seriousness of commitment with seriousness in its emotional sense. If you look at small children, they are phenomenal learners who learn largely through play. They focus their atten-tion on things that interest, amuse or puzzle them, and can surprise adults with their ability to concentrate. Once they solve the puzzle, learn the skill or simply find something else catching their attention, they move on. They are rarely serious in the grim and determined way adults can be.

Playful, experimental discovery learning is a good model for us as adults too. In fact, Gallwey found that he could help his pupils stay in the state of relaxed awareness that helped them most if he got them to focus on things that were (a) observable, (b) interesting and (c) relevant – just the kinds of things that get children involved. There's more about this in Chapters 3, 6 and 8.

This kind of learning is learning by doing: it's experimental, it focuses on what works and abandons what doesn't. It's not judgemental (good/bad, better/worse, success/failure). Sometimes it results in pursuing a task for a considerable length of time, sometimes it results in abandoning it rapidly and finding something different. In coaching, it's useful to trust your senses and your gut feelings. You can choose to override them, but be aware that there can be a high cost. If you got the half-pass right the first time, why do it another five times? Equally, if you got it wrong, why repeat it again and again unless you change something? There's a saying in NLP: '*If you always do what you've always done, you'll always get what you've always got*'. 'Ought', 'must' and 'should' are rarely helpful in coaching, whether ourselves or others.

Coaching focuses on action and on goals. So does skill-learning. There is always another refinement to make, another goal to aim for. Coaching also allows us to recap, or even to go back. Sometimes, as a dressage judge, I see horses and riders 'doing the movements', but with some fundamental problem showing up. The most common, for example, are lack of softness and round-ness. Even if the horse can do accurate transitions and perform some sort of shoulder-in or half-pass, stiffness in his neck and back may give away short-cuts in his earlier training. It's no disgrace, but rather a tribute to responsible riding, if you take your horse's stiffness or hollowness – even if it's temporary – as a signal that it's time to go back to the basics again. As your own coach, work with what *needs* to be done, not what 'ought' to be done. And if you or your horse feel bored, do something different. Go for a hack, do some jumping, work over trotting poles, loose school. Break the pattern that has become sour. Good work comes from vitality, not from staleness.

Taking Responsibility and Accepting Yourself

Take responsibility for yourself and accept yourself *as opposed to being passive or dependent or self-undermining.*

Riding is about a relationship, but like relationships with other human beings this one will be more productive if you take responsibility for your share in it and work with yourself, rather than hoping that your horse, or your teacher, or other external circumstances, will make things happen for you. It's hard some-times to say: 'That went wrong, what can I do about it?' But even when what happened wasn't your fault, taking responsibility for how you respond puts you back in charge again.

H ORSES, LIKE PEOPLE, have off days. If you recognize this and blame your horse for a disappointing session, you've put yourself into a powerless position. However, if you recognize it and think about how you could change your response to harmonize with him, or to regain his attention, you are taking control. You will feel better, and therefore you will give him a message of confidence and decisiveness instead of one of helplessness and despondency. As a herd animal, which kind of leadership is he more likely to respond to?

OR PERHAPS SOMETHING goes wrong at the yard, or you're unhappy about the approach your teacher is taking. The easiest response is to grumble. The hardest – but the most productive – response is to work out what you really want and speak to someone about it. You may feel nervous about telling or asking, but the discomfort of doing this is likely to be relatively short-lived, and the payoff well worth it. Waiting for others to change prolongs the discomfort and makes it feel even worse, because you now feel powerless as well as aggrieved.

Monitoring Yourself Through Heightened Awareness

Monitor yourself through a heightened awareness, through assessing how your actions may be experienced by your horse, and through curious and objective self-observation *as opposed to only seeing things from your own point of view, or ignoring your own feelings and views because you think those of your trainer or horse are more important.*

NLP has identified two key abilities that make for good communication – and good riding is good communication. The first one is the ability to notice and monitor small details and recognize how they may be relevant. NLP describes this as having **sensory acuity**.

FOR EXAMPLE, my husband Leo was watching me ride on one occasion, and noticed that my weight seemed to be slipping to the outside. The obvious correction was to put more weight into my inside stirrup, which I tried hard to do. After a few more minutes Leo said: 'Stop a moment. Let's just look at your stirrup leathers.' The inside one was a hole shorter than the outside one, so of course I was being tipped to the outside, however hard I tried. Leo is very good at monitoring differences of this sort (he's the kind of person who gets the picture hook exactly in the middle of the chimney-breast without measuring). NLP calls this process **calibration**, and the ability to calibrate differences and changes gives you high quality information to work with. Calibrating your horse's responses, and the fine details of your own behaviour, is a delightful skill to develop, because it adds so much joy and subtlety to the conversations you have together.

The second key ability is that of understanding how a situation can seem from different points of view. NLP calls this **taking different perceptual positions**. There are three of these:

Being in **first position** is evaluating how things are to you, inside yourself, looking out through your own eyes. Usually this feels great when things go well, but not when you're stuck or when things go badly.

Taking **second position** involves imagining how things are for someone else. In riding, the someone whose experience it's most useful for you to be able to imagine in this way is your horse. Taking his position as you interact with him offers you an important way of checking up on your own behaviour through his eyes and feelings. What you get out of this is a way of understanding and predicting his responses to you. This, in turn, helps you get the messages clearer for him.

Taking **third position** involves viewing a situation in which you're involved as if you were an outsider, a fly on the wall. It gives you a viewpoint that is detached from emotion but is at the same time interested and concerned. It's a really useful check when things go wrong, or for assessing technical progress, or for future planning.

In discussing this issue I've used the phrases 'viewing', 'looking out through your own eyes' and other visual allusions. This may be how you do it – you literally see things in your own mind. But I could have said 'stepping into someone else's shoes', because like many people you may 'feel it how it is' in your mind rather than seeing it. And you could be one of a smaller number of people who 'hear what's going on' or think about 'getting on the same wavelength' – in other words, you are processing internally through your sense of hearing rather than, or as much as, through seeing or feeling.

Whichever sense or senses you favour in your own thinking, the ability to take different perceptual positions is a key skill in communicating effectively. Knowing about this skill, and practising to increase your flexibility in using it, provides a great tool for self-coaching.

Developing a Relaxed Focus

Develop a relaxed focus on what is happening here and now; be curious about what is observable, interesting and relevant *as opposed to thinking so much about the future or going over the past that you miss out on what is happening now and lose opportunities to influence it.*

Where are you in your head right now? Are you really engaged in reading this – to the point where perhaps you've ceased to hear traffic in the street outside, or where the others around you have had to repeat what they're saying to get your attention? Are you half-thinking of something else? Perhaps something you've read has set you off thinking about what happened last week when... or how you've never been able to... Or perhaps something you read caught your interest and you were off imagining how you could try it out next time you ride. Our minds are the ultimate space and time travellers.

Having some ability to monitor and control this is another key to coaching. If you're off in last week or tomorrow, there's less of you available here and now. And when you're riding, this can be either a problem (if you're 'absent' for too long), or an asset (if you can use this skill rapidly to monitor results and aims or to calibrate differences from last time, last month or last year).

Timothy Gallwey found that the most effective state for performance was one of 'relaxed awareness'. Although he uses the word 'relaxed', it is clear that he means 'not tense, not trying too hard'. All athletes need tone in their muscles – but tension works against the effortless, unconscious ease being aimed for. Muscles that are toned but not tense are swifter, subtler and more effective in doing what is needed than 'trying' muscles; and the mind translates into action much better through them. And this kind of non-judgemental attentiveness to what's happening here and now puts you in a state that's uncluttered by 'baggage', so you can react rapidly and appropriately. For many people, being truly 'here-and-now' in relaxed, mutual attentiveness with their horse is one of the greatest pleasures of riding.

Being Rigorous Without Pressurizing

Be rigorous, but without putting pressure on yourself or your horse *as opposed to losing purpose or, alternatively, driving the partnership to achieve.*

Gallwey spotted that pressure, whether it comes from outside (trainers or specific targets such as competitions), or from inside (Self One internal dialogue), puts the muscles into tense, 'trying' mode rather than relaxed, attentive mode. Our minds are also less receptive under pressure because we're trying to run 'oughts', 'musts' and 'shoulds' alongside the open attentiveness we need for effective monitoring. Yet, clearly, slopping along in a daze won't get us anywhere, either. That kind of absent-mindedness takes us out of our relaxed focus in another way.

What we need to develop instead is a habit of being rigorous without pressure – being involved, attentive, committed, aware of ourselves, our horse, what's going on and how it relates to our desired outcomes. It's easier to be

rigorous in a curiosity frame rather than a success/failure frame, because we can use what happens as important feedback to guide how we respond. Does it work – or not? What happens if I do this instead? How might it be if…?

With this frame of mind, we can truly operate as our own coaches, taking ourselves forward. This is a noticing state, a questioning state, an experimental state. It's the best kind of state to help us realize our own potential, and thereby to release our ability to help our horses realize theirs.

Truly here and now in relaxed mutual attentiveness – Nicky and Lucinda.

What this Demands of You and Your Horse

Setting targets for yourself and coaching yourself to work towards them in this highly attentive and thoughtful way is often hard work. It takes persistence to concentrate like this – which may seem the very opposite of the permissive and relaxed focus I've been advocating. If you have ever practised meditation or relaxation techniques you may have wondered what to do when your mind wanders: most teachers will advise you to accept the wandering thoughts, let them go and simply bring yourself back to your intended focus again. It's much the same with the self-coaching approach. Losing concentration may tell you something is too hard, that you're tired, that your horse needs to relax or perhaps have something explained to him in smaller, simpler stages. The important point to realize is that *whatever happens, is potentially useful information – provided you stay outside the blame-frame.* And if you do get into judgemental mode, notice it, be curious about it and let it go. Don't, above all, blame yourself for self-blame!

The curiosity-frame soon becomes a habit of its own, and it gets easier to stay attentive. In its own way, it can be an exacting discipline – but one which is both positive and productive of new learning. In my experience, and that of people I've worked with, it adds a level of wonder and fascination, of never-ending exploration and amazement, to this already miraculous thing we're engaged in – having an ongoing conversation with a member of another species.

'Involved in a process' – Nikki and Beamish.

Achieving your goals may seem to take longer because you are taking things gradually rather than forcing the pace. But the journey to them is surer, truer and more enjoyable every step of the way. No short cuts means no blind alleys. Paying attention means you notice and can enjoy every little step towards your achievement rather than having to wait until your major goal materializes. You're involved in a process, not dominated by a product. You get to choose, to plan, to investigate, to discover. Every session can bring its own puzzles and its own rewards. And because you're more relaxed, so is your horse. You can have better conversations together: you can listen to each other, and whisper rather than shout at each other. Riding becomes fun again. Even dealing with problems can often become intriguing rather than dispiriting. This is what you get when you take a coaching approach. And this book is going to show you how.

2

Taking a Coaching Approach – the Basic Assumptions

I N THE PREVIOUS CHAPTER I described some of the core features of an NLP coaching approach, and now I'm going to explore how key coaching assumptions can help us in our riding.

Truth, Assumptions and Presuppositions

When we believe something, we tend to act as if it were 'true', regardless of whether it's a fact (for example, London is bigger than Yeovil), or whether it's a theory (for example, Warmbloods are best at dressage). So beliefs have a powerful effect on shaping our thoughts, feelings and behaviour. Assumptions are beliefs which come from past experience and from formal and informal teaching, and which we use to guide us in managing the present and anticipating the future. They act as filters which help us to make sense of what happens, and we can't manage life without them. If you can remember your first day at work, or your first day at school, or the first time you rode, you may remember how much information seemed to be coming at you and how hard it was to make sense of it. As time progressed, you rapidly began to build up ways of sorting and making sense of that experience. You grouped information into clusters and under headings. You recognized patterns. You began to be able to anticipate what was coming.

As mentioned earlier, the NLP word for these guiding assumptions is presuppositions. There are some presuppositions of which we are consciously aware, but all of us operate on the basis of many we are less aware of. And these hidden presuppositions can shape things – often quite powerfully – without our realizing it. For example, assuming the best isn't always going to be borne out in the event, any more than assuming the worst. But both presuppositions will have decisive effects, because we will act accordingly. They are our guidelines for action, and for interpreting what occurs.

One way of uncovering hidden presuppositions is to ask yourself from time to time 'What am I assuming here?' For example, if your horse doesn't do what you ask, do you:

- hit him *(assuming that he's being naughty)*

- repeat the instruction *(assuming that he isn't paying attention)*

- think of another way of explaining what you want *(assuming that he doesn't understand)*?

None of these assumptions is inherently 'right' or 'better' – but do you know what your evidence was for assuming that a particular response was the result of naughtiness, inattention or confusion? Checking for evidence is one way of ensuring that the assumption underlying your response had a specific foundation.

If you can't ascertain what the evidence was, or if – when you're honest with yourself – you recognize that you often think of your horse as, for example, being lazy, ask yourself whether you tend to think of horses *in general* as lazy… or even whether you think that *people* lack motivation unless they are being pushed or have specific incentives. Both such generalized beliefs will tell you that a presupposition is at work, acting as a filter for how you interpret the actions of others, and also guiding your own.

Once we know what our presuppositions are, we can look at the way they shape things. If we discover that they may be limiting what we can achieve, we can begin to wonder about what would be less limiting, and start to make changes. More information means more choice.

Enabling Presuppositions

I'd like to outline some of the enabling presuppositions which I've learnt from my experience as an NLP practitioner and coach, who also happens to be a rider and judge. These are presuppositions which have been found to make communication with others more effective, and to help people achieve outcomes that matter to them. They are assumptions which I find helpful when I'm riding on my own, which form the basis of work I do helping others, and which underpin much of the material in this book.

Effective Communication

Effective communication involves dialogue and negotiation. As riders, we are involved with two, often three, kinds of communication: with our horse; with ourselves; with our trainer. If we presuppose that this involves dialogue and negotiation, this takes us in different directions from those we'd go in if we presupposed that riding simply or largely involved giving and receiving instructions. In my experience, we get further if we think of our interactions as two-way conversations. This is how most of the great riding masters have described it, and the label 'conversation' reflects the subtle mutual responsive-ness which characterizes both good riding and good teaching. If you presuppose that riding is a conversation, you'll be carrying over some assump-tions and guidelines from everyday conversation between people into what you believe and expect from interaction between people and horses. For exam-ple, that the rider needs sensitivity to appreciate how the horse receives what the rider is communicating, and how he understands it; and the consequential need for flexibility, to ensure that the rider's communications are adjusted and refined to make it easier for the horse to understand them.

If you are having lessons, you need similar skills to gain the most from your teacher. You will have to process their comments and instructions at the same time as being attentive to your horse (think about the difficulty of trying to hold two conversations at once!), and sometimes you will have to 'translate' what the teacher is saying in your own mind – or ask them to say it differently – in order to understand it fully. Their goals may not always be the same as yours, and you may have to renegotiate the purpose of the training. Or they may go faster – or slower – than you would like. Do you say something about this, or put up with it? Framed like this, the situation invites you into negotia-tion. (The same issues will arise the other way round, of course, if you are the teacher.)

What about the third kind of communication? Sometimes we're aware that we're in conflict with ourselves, or talking to ourselves. There is often a lot going on in there! **Internal dialogue** (as NLP calls it) happens much more often than we realize – and it can be very powerful. Internal conversations may not always take the form of words. If you do a rein-back which is reasonably fluent, but notice through your seat and through checking how parallel you are to the side of the school that your horse isn't quite straight, and therefore feel disappointed, this wordless internal experience may be just as powerful in undermining your confidence as if you'd actually said to yourself 'that really wasn't good enough'. There is a communication and a response involved – and both are taking place inside you! And if you often take a critical attitude to yourself, or are always shifting your goal posts so that you never rest and take delight in what you've done, the effects of your internal conversations may stack up to limit what you can achieve.

NLP has shown us that the most effective kinds of communication are those where both parties gain something – where the situation is 'win-win'. And as riders, that's a useful aim to have. If we presuppose that we're engaged in dialogue and negotiation, we can try to make the dialogues productive for every-one involved. Having a win-win situation as our outcome will tend to enhance our attentiveness to how our horse, or trainer, or our own self, responds.

LET'S IMAGINE THAT it's a windy autumn day. The horse needs exercising, but trees are being blown about and his friends are cavorting in the field – not very conducive to serious schooling. You get out the trotting poles and place them down one side of the school, and you intersperse working over them with your 'more serious' dressage. He enjoys himself, you have fun, and his trot gains more suspension and rhythm – win-win.

States – Yours and Your Horse's

The state you (and your horse) are in determines what you can achieve. 'I'm not in a fit state to try anything ambitious today.' 'All I'm fit for is a quiet hack.' 'He's all wound up because he hasn't been out of his box for a couple of days.' Comments like these show that we all recognize the importance of the state we're in and its effects on what we want to do.

In NLP, a **state** is a single mind-body experience made up of several elements: emotion, physiology, mental processing. In any one day we experi-ence many states, some of which are marked enough to notice while others are either fleeting enough or familiar enough to escape our attention. As the comments above show, we know that certain states are more or less appropriate for particular activities or aims.

IF YOU'RE MISERABLE, you aren't likely to enjoy an evening in the pub – unless, perhaps, meeting your friends and having a drink helps you change to a cheerful state. In that case, you may go home in a markedly different state from the one in which you started the evening.

If you're tired, your mind-body state is going to make it hard to concentrate on something that requires attention to detail or persistent repetition. Yet many of us turn up at the yard after a hard day's work expecting – or at least hoping – to school our horses effectively.

And what about the horse? He has states of his own – and he can also 'catch' states from his rider, because states have their characteristic postures, tensions, reactions and probably even smells. This is one reason why many horses get wound up in competition, even if they are not bothered by being transported to a less familiar place. They pick up the 'competition state' the rider is in. It's my belief that horses sense human emotions but are often confused by them – it's a kind of sensory overload for them. And many of the professional riders

A windy day. Lolly started off excited and inattentive, but matching his forward energy with lots of cantering helped us to reach a position where we could work together with harmony and concentration.

and trainers I've talked to have stressed independently how important it is, for just this reason, to leave emotion aside when you ride.

Chapter 8 looks at states more fully, and shows you how states of certain kinds can be really helpful to you and your horse. It also explains how to recognize and change states so that you manage them rather than being managed by them.

Representing Issues to Yourself

Knowing your own ways of representing something to yourself in your mind allows you to target how you coach yourself more effectively.

We all use the word 'think' as though it means the same thing to each of us; but one of the early, and most important, discoveries of NLP was that this isn't the case. (The same is true of the word 'imagine'.) For some people, thinking involves making pictures – still or moving – in their heads. These may be coloured, black-and-white, close up or far away, bright or pastel, sharp or fuzzy – and of course these qualities will affect the meaning and impact of the picture so far as the individual is concerned. Someone else, on the other hand, will have few pictures but plenty of physical memories and imagined feelings instead. Thinking of a good ride, in their experience, may be almost like doing it: they'll have a sense of movement, rhythm, orientation in space, pressure, temperature, etc. Yet another person may be more 'in tune' with sound and do much of their thinking through this.

NLP calls these ways of processing **representational systems** because they are the ways in which we re-present our experience to ourselves internally. (The initial 'presentation' is the first impact of experience on us as we interact with the external world.)

There are five representational systems: **visual**, **auditory**, **kinesthetic**, **olfactory** (smell) and **gustatory** (taste). Most people can use all of these, but each of us tends to favour one or two. The implication for self-coaching is that, if we know and work within our favoured system(s), we can communicate more effectively with ourselves.

IF YOU'RE FEELING anxious about something, with a sinking heart, churning stomach and dry mouth whenever you imagine it, your kinesthetic representational system is giving you a bad time today about something that either happened last week or may be about to happen tomorrow. It can be nearly as bad as the real thing – sometimes, it can even be worse! If you want to change this experience, it won't really help much to tell yourself off for being silly, since that involves internal dialogue, which is a different form of representation (auditory). Equally, a would-be helpful suggestion from someone else that you 'see yourself doing it safely and successfully' won't really connect with you because that's visual: if you don't 'do' pictures it won't help you. You are going to make positive changes most easily and effectively if you work within the representational system in which you're experiencing the problem – in this case, kinesthetic. Chapter 8 looks at how you can manage this in more detail.

How You Frame Things

How you frame something (a situation, a process, a problem or goal) will shape what you do and will be conveyed to your horse through the mind-body connection.

LET'S START WITH AN example. An event horse has to be obedient, balanced, on the aids, capable of changing speed and stride-length rapidly. Does this sound a bit like dressage? Yet many eventers see dressage as a necessary evil which has to be gone through if they are to do what they really enjoy, which is riding and jumping across country. Some event riders get anxious and tense about the dressage phase, just as others do about showjumping. Yet a horse who can make multiple

An event horse has to be obedient, balanced, on the aids...Sean with Harry.

adjustments of speed, gait, balance and direction across rough terrain will find a level, springy dressage arena easy to work on. So why so many problems? One reason is that the way the rider frames dressage in his or her mind – in this case, as something foreign and difficult – is communicated subtly to the horse through the rider's state and behaviour.

The way we frame something in our minds shapes the experience just as a picture frame shapes the image it contains. A different frame produces a different overall effect, even though the content is the same. So it's worthwhile examining how we frame our riding and checking whether this particular frame works with or against the outcome we want. When you change the frame, you change the meaning and impact of the experience.

In this book I'm going to concentrate on some kinds of framing rather than others. In particular, I'm interested in how a frame of curiosity helps us into a state of calm yet rigorous inquiry which produces information that we can use, in contrast to the way that the success-failure frame tends to pressurize us and make us more tense and self-critical. As I mentioned earlier, Timothy Gallwey found that when his pupils were in a 'trying' frame, they were not only anxious about how they were doing, they also generated muscle tension which interfered with suppleness and speed of reaction – and this in turn interfered with their performance. On the other hand, the frame that he called 'relaxed awareness' encouraged them to notice important and often subtle details which, in turn, helped them to improve easily and without tension – significantly, he also noted that in this state they became automatically self-correcting.

WORKING WITH A RIDER one day, I asked her what she wanted to achieve in our session together. 'I want to stop perching on the saddle', she said. I told her that as I didn't know what she meant by perching I'd like her to ride around me in a circle showing me perching and not-perching alternately. Without any hesitation she did this, changing her posture every few strides. This amazed her – and became the basis of a playful and very productive session, in which she discovered how she did perching and not-perching, and was able to make the not-perching more habitual and extend it into the other gaits. This was in marked contrast to the more serious and concentrated dressage lesson she had expected, but in this state of non-pressured awareness she was able to achieve something she had previously found difficult to sustain however hard she 'tried'. (For a fuller account of this session, see Framing in Action, following Chapter 7.)

How You Filter Information

We always have to filter information from the outside world in order to make sense of it, so knowing our habitual filters is an important means of understanding our characteristic strengths and weaknesses – and of allowing us to develop our range of skills.

Perhaps you have had the experience of being abroad and listening to a language you don't understand. You are bombarded with information, but you don't have a way of sorting it to make sense of it. All of us had this experience, of course, when we were very young, and the ability to talk fluently that we now have was built on the human skill of recognizing patterns, both of sound and structure.

Sorting information according to learnt patterns is both an essential tool and a potential trap, because we can also distort the information by making it fit into an expected pattern.

One of the most exciting discoveries of NLP was that people interpret their experience according to a number of internal sorting mechanisms, and that these profoundly affect what each of us thinks of as the 'reality' of our experience. The same events will have different meanings for different people, according to the way they each characteristically make sense of their experience. That's why NLP calls these processes **meta-programmes**: they are recognizable and repeating structures (programmes) for organizing our experience at a high (meta-) level rather than a detailed level.

THE JOKE ABOUT the person who thinks the bottle is half-empty and the one who thinks of it as half-full shows how we recognize this process in everyday life. The 'truth' about the bottle depends on how you look at it – and that in turn depends on your sorting patterns.

In Chapter 5 I'm going to show how these important and fascinating sorting mechanisms affect our ability to motivate ourselves and manage our experience; and how knowing this can help us to understand and work with our own patterning. Many meta-programmes have now been identified, but I'm going to concentrate on just a few of the key ones. And in Chapter 6 I'm going to explore a new idea – that the way our horses behave seems to show that they, too, make sense of their experience through meta-programmes. Even though they don't think like us, and there can be no hard evidence for this in their case, I think it can be useful for us as riders to act *as-if* they did. When we do so, we gain a valuable tool for harnessing their individual motivation and planning their training in ways which make it easier for them to learn.

An understanding of meta-programmes is crucial in good communication: when we know how someone characteristically makes sense of their experience we can present things to them in ways that they are more likely to understand. We can use this knowledge to get more from our teachers, our horses, and ourselves.

Modelling

Modelling is the process of finding out in detail how someone does something – whether it's something external, like behaviour – which can be observed – or something internal like thinking or feeling, which we can only find out about by asking. (And, of course, behaviour itself is usually accompanied by sequences of thought and feeling.)

Modelling is the key to skill development. Modelling what works gives you important information about how it works. Modelling what doesn't work so well tells you what changes need to be made, and where. We can model both ourselves and others.

When you ask someone the modelling question 'How do you do that?', and keep asking until you get really detailed information, you are gaining recipes for how to do what they do. Thus modelling is a great tool for learning.

Like many complex physical skills, riding has developed a huge body of detailed information which seems to provide such recipes. But when we take an NLP approach we begin to realize that many of these recipes don't go into enough detail for us to use them with a reliable prediction of success.

EVERYONE KNOWS THAT you need to keep your heels down when you ride. Many people know that the reason for this is that, when your heels are down, your calf muscles are automatically stretched and toned so that they can be effective in aiding your horse. Yet most riders have difficulty in keeping their heels down, and may take years to achieve the correct position. The key modelling word here is 'how' you, or I, or someone we admire, would be able to place and keep the heels down. In *Schooling Problems Solved with NLP* I described working with one rider who found that, if she remembered some special red shoes she had when she was little, it was easier for her toes to come up and her heels to go down. Another rider I worked with found that she thought of her current, horizontal foot position as being 5 out of 10 and the position she and her teacher were aiming for as 7 out of 10. When I asked her to think her way from 5 to 7 her feet naturally assumed – and kept – the position she wanted.

These riders had very different ways of representing this particular positioning to themselves. Using a coaching approach meant that I could help them find out exactly how they could reorganize their positioning. For one, a visual memory was the key: for the other, it was the idea of progressive numbers. I didn't know this initially – and neither did they until I asked them the 'how' question.

Modelling can be really helpful in understanding and changing how we feel, too. If you know *how* you 'do' being frightened, or how you 'do' being confident, then you have a pattern you can use as a template to alter or construct your experience. For example, you might make a detailed comparison between what happens for you when you're anxious about something, and when you expect things to go well: what are the key differences? Altering some or all of these will help you bring about the changes you want.

ONE RIDER I WORKED with was frightened of being run away with. When we looked at how she experienced this fear, it became clear that she ran a kind of video in her head, and that she stopped it – quite understandably – at the point when she got really frightened. Of course, the horror movies she was running made her fear get worse and worse. So I asked her to continue the video rather than stopping it, to add in a sequence that included using the knowledge she had about turning and slowing a horse, using her seat and posture to calm him and bring him back under control again. She had this information, and the skill to use it – but she hadn't put it into her horror movie. Once she did, she could continue the movie until she got to a safe and successful ending. Doing this a number of times when she found herself imagining the worst deconstructed the old pattern, and she lost her fear. This enabled her to get on and start enjoying her riding again.

Feedback from Behaviour

Feedback is essential to progress. Behaviour is feedback. 'Failure' is also valuable feedback. We can use feedback to feed forward.

When we're learning something or working towards a goal, we need to know how we're doing: we need feedback. Feedback comes from the comments of observers (friends or trainers) and from our own recognition of how what we're doing matches up with the aim or the ideal we're working towards – in other words, what happens in response to our actions.

Let's take the example of asking your horse to halt.

Did he halt when asked? Yes.

Did he halt obediently? Well, a bit reluctantly.

Was he straight? No.

Was he engaged into the halt? The trainer said his hocks were out behind.

This is all feedback. Having this information means that you can adjust what you do and try to make it better next time. But often, however 'true' it may be, feedback makes you feel bad – and that makes it harder, not easier, for you to do better next time.

NLP coaching helps us take a different approach to feedback. Because of its emphasis on 'how', it puts us in a state of curiosity and inquiry that helps out even when things do go wrong. This state helps us to stay outside the framework of good/bad judgements, which are usually emotionally loaded. Let's run the example again using this approach, and discover what answers this gives:

Did he halt when asked? Yes, because I shifted my weight back and closed my fists.

Did he halt obediently? No, because I hadn't used half-halts to prepare him and get him balanced so that it would be easy for him to stop.

Was he straight? No, because my weight was unevenly distributed and one leg was stronger and more down into the stirrup than the other.

Was he engaged into the halt? No, because I hadn't closed my legs enough to bring his hocks under him and get him to 'sit': I stopped the front end and the back end wasn't under full control.

This may seem a rather low-level example, yet plenty of good dressage tests are marked down because riders haven't gathered and used this kind of feedback. Equally, many a gate-stop on a hack can involve wrestling or overshooting the ideal spot from which to manage the catch because of an ineffective halting technique. Seeking feedback rather than just slapping a good/bad label on what happens means that you help yourself gather the information you need in order to become better and more effective. Feedback then becomes feed-forward – you know what you need to do next time.

There's another benefit to this approach: it makes riding (or any other activity you look at in this way) even more fascinating. One of the delights of riding is the detailed discussion we get into with ourselves and with other riders; the replay of good moments; the imagining of how we'd like things to be. These become even more enjoyable, and much more productive, when we model what's going on and use feedback from what happens to feed forward to the future.

Feedback from Curiosity and Questions

You get more feedback from questions than from statements; from curiosity rather than from success/failure judgements.

It will be clear by now that coaching relies heavily on questions – both between people and in our conversations with ourselves. The effect of a statement is to close things down; the effect of a question is to expand and explore the issue further. 'Halt not square or engaged' on the judge's sheet may leave you feeling disappointed, angry or helpless. Asking yourself the kind of questions I've just run through about what happened, how it happened and what things could be changed puts you back in control again.

But there's another kind of question that coaching uses which can be even more fascinating and productive – questions that set you off thinking about something you hadn't thought of before, or didn't know you had the answer to.

WORKING WITH MY FRIEND Nikki one day, on the problem of her 'dead left hand', I asked her first how it was different from the right hand, and where the differences were coming from. All we knew to start with was that the left hand was lower, less active and less responsive than the right. My questions made her search for answers – and she said that the left hand felt more wooden and less alive than the right – 'like a marionette'. When she tracked back from the hand, this difference went all the way up to the shoulder. Then I asked her another question: 'How can your left hand learn from your right hand what it needs to do in order to match the right one and be as responsive?' I didn't know the answer, but the question produced another internal search – and she found herself making the adjustments she needed without knowing what they had to be or how she was making them. This was what Timothy Gallwey found in his inner coaching work: asking the question was often enough to produce automatic self-correction in his pupils. And because it was organized at an inner, unconscious level, and organized in response to internal processing rather than as a result of 'telling' or 'teaching' from outside, the changes were more lasting.

This kind of search question – where we don't have the information at a conscious level – sets off mental processes that take place beyond awareness.

Gallwey makes the point that, normally, when we adjust our positioning or movement, we rely naturally on unconscious organization: we just don't have all the information about how it's done at a conscious level (if we had to do it consciously, we'd have little mental space for anything else!). Therefore, it doesn't make sense to try to make these adjustments consciously – yet that's how much of skill-learning is traditionally taught and organized. No wonder we get so anxious and overwhelmed at times. What is most useful is to do consciously that which can best be done consciously – and to do unconsciously that which can only, or more effectively, be done that way. And search questions are an important way of engaging unconscious processing, which we can learn to do for ourselves as well as for others.

Less is More

When you watch a really outstanding rider, you can hardly see their aiding. They seem to be at one with the horse, like the mythical centaurs who were half human and half horse. Thought and intention simply flow into action. That's what we are aiming for – however far we know we are from that ideal at the moment.

'Less is more'.
Marisian and Prudie.

I'd like you consider this same idea from another angle. Remember that your horse is sensitive enough to feel exactly where a single fly lands on his skin, and responsive enough to flick it off. Why would he need thumping heels and tight reins to tell him what you want from him? Rather than believing that invisible aids are attainable only after years of training and experience, how would it alter things for you and for him if you believed from the start that you could communicate with tiny signals, and that he had the capacity to respond to them? One exciting possibility might be that you could train him progressively to respond to lighter and lighter, quieter and quieter, subtler and subtler aids.

This brings us back to the matter of information again. We need to know what signals the horse is going to understand, and that means knowing about his physiology, his previous training and his individual nature. We also need the mental and physical skills to make our signalling precise and appropriate. Reading, watching videos of the masters, talking with knowledgeable people, watching excellent riders and having good coaching can all add to this body of information. But it is just as important to become aware of how you signal and how the horse responds – and to experiment to discover how little you can do, how quietly you can 'speak' to him with your aiding. Doing this requires that you and he pay attention to each other. But, paradoxically, shouting aids – like a shouting voice – tend to produce 'deafness'. Riders with busy legs that flap every stride produce horses who are dead to the leg. A rider who gives a single, clear leg aid – and follows it with a tap of the whip if the horse doesn't respond – and is then still, trains the horse to understand that 'when the rider's leg comes on, it's telling me something and I need to respond'.

I WAS COACHING A RIDER with a talented horse and she said that, even though the horse was quite successful in tests, he was often tense when she asked him to work at home in the shortened outline he needed for his level of competition. She wondered whether his reluctance, especially at the beginning of a schooling session, might be his way of saying that his muscles weren't warmed-up enough for him to shorten and engage comfortably – but she felt that she 'ought' to be 'schooling him properly' and that this meant 'picking him up' and 'asking him to go forward more'. I suggested that she listen to what he seemed to be saying, work for a while in the way that he offered, and then reassess. After about fifteen minutes of rhythmical deep work he began to engage more and to offer a shorter frame and lighter forehand. He brought himself into the correct outline she had felt she needed to ask for. She turned to me and said 'I've been shouting at him, and I only needed to whisper'.

The axiom 'less is more' isn't a licence to do nothing. Instead, it is a permission to consider what is the least you need to do in order to achieve what you want. Your goals are still important – but if you can achieve them with fewer and subtler aids, less pressure on yourself and the horse, and through playful experimentation rather than conscientious, effort-filled 'trying', you and your horse will achieve a calmer, more delightful, more effective way of communicating with each other – and that, in turn, will make the work you do together more successful.

PART 2

Getting Started

3

Becoming More Aware

IF YOU'RE GOING TO BE REALLY effective as your own coach, observation will be one of your most essential skills: rapid, detailed monitoring of what's going on, both externally and internally. When the developers of NLP studied people who were brilliant at communicating, they found that one thing these outstanding communicators had in common was that they were great observers. They noticed everything about the people they worked with. Not just the content of what was said but *how* it was said: tone, pitch, pace, hesitations, metaphors. Not just facial expressions but body movement and stillness, muscle tone, skin colour and the way it changed – and how these factors related to what was being said at the time. They noticed patterns of behaviour and reaction. They connected today's information with last week's – and last month's – and with information they'd been given about things that happened years before. They had learnt to watch and to listen really intently, and to make connections between the different kinds and levels of information they received.

Your riding teacher may have similar abilities. An astute teacher may comment on what your horse is doing, and how that relates to subtle details of how you are riding him, with a speed and accuracy that astonish – and perhaps sometimes dismay – you. How did she notice that, you may think. And why didn't I notice it?

Developing Sensory Acuity

NLP calls this kind of observational skill sensory acuity because it isn't simply visual. Really good observers use all their senses to gather information. A good trainer is likely to be using their ears to monitor rhythm and energy (the horse's footfalls, his breathing patterns), and drawing on an ability to recreate various physical sensations mentally, in order to assess what your horse's movement feels like and how you are sensing and carrying out your riding. NLP calls this 'feeling' sense kinesthetic, and kinesthetic awareness is another word for the 'feel' that characterizes good riders and trainers. I think it likely that good trainers also, to some extent, feel empathetically what the horse is experiencing: they do more than see interrupted rhythm or stiffness in the back – they have a *felt* sense of the way the horse is holding himself and what it's like to move with a disturbed sequence. Certainly, they often have a felt sense of what their human pupil is experiencing, as you can sometimes tell if you watch them tapping or even bouncing in rhythm, or mirroring the way the pupil's body is turning or their weight is shifting.

We all have the potential to notice these kinds of things, and we can train ourselves to improve our ability to do so. When we do, we give ourselves so much more to work with, and so much more leverage by which to become effective. Perhaps even more importantly, we increase our ability to help ourselves.

M Y FRIEND, DEBBY, told me that when she first saw Charles de Kunffy teaching she was struck by the way he got his pupils to 'sculpt' their legs into the correct position. She knew that her own leg position wasn't yet as correct as it could be, so she decided she would do the same sculpting for herself. So, when she rode on her own, she would check and correct her leg position every few minutes. She did this consistently, every ride, for some time, until correct positioning became an automatic habit.

EXERCISE

Take a comment your teacher made recently about your horse or your riding, and which you found an accurate and helpful observation. Next time you ride, check up on this at intervals. Is it happening again? Do you need to make a correction? If it was something that was praised, are you doing it today? Could you be doing it more?

This may sound like a lot of work, but really it's just focused dedication – to yourself and your horse. You already put a lot of effort into your riding, and perhaps make sacrifices of time, money and other opportunities to do so. Why not make that effort and those sacrifices pay off even more, and in a way which gives you more independence? That way, you can really make the most of what you learn, whether it's face-to-face through lessons or through other means of learning, like books and videos. Become an experimenter! As you do so, you'll find out what works for you and what doesn't. In turn, you'll be able to identify those issues that need an outsider's help and thus make the most of your teaching, rather than having your trainer comment yet again on the need for a stiller hand, or a deeper seat. This way, your lessons become a springboard for work you can take forward on your own, a diagnostic clinic for new or intractable problems, a place for brainstorming different approaches and for benchmarking progress. And if you compete, it will help you to frame results or test sheets in the same way, rather than experiencing competition as an all-powerful, mysteriously correct judgement. A competition is a snapshot, and like any snapshot it may catch you in a glorious, or inglorious moment. It's not a final truth.

What to Look Out For

In order to gather information, we need to know what we're looking for. Here are some ways of guiding your search, and for filtering and sorting what you find.

First, decide whether you want to improve a technical skill or solve a specific problem that's occurring.

Second, ask yourself if your focus is going to be yourself, or your horse.

If your focus is on you – for example, working on your position in some way – give yourself permission to ask less of your horse than you would do normally. Stick with simple shapes, basic gaits. You don't have to let him slop about, but don't distract yourself from your main aim by having to monitor the exact angle of his shoulder-in or whether that eight-metre volte really is eight metres. Focus on your own needs and save that issue for another day.

Taking Different Perceptual Positions

If your focus is on your horse, start by imagining yourself into his world, his experience. As we saw in Chapter 1, NLP calls this 'taking second position'. (Being in first position means we're primarily paying attention to our own experience, and being in third position is taking a concerned observer's view of a situation we're involved in – it's the fly-on-the-wall approach: detached from the emotions of the situation but with a well-wishing attitude to those who are feeling them. We can benefit in different ways from taking each of these positions.)

When you're wondering why your horse doesn't seem to understand what you want, or why he is getting anxious or resistant, it's very helpful to step into second position with him. What sense is he likely to be making of what's going on – including what you're telling him?

I TALKED WITH ONE rider whose five-year-old horse had a delightfully forward-going attitude. The youngster was enthusiastic. She enjoyed being ridden, both out hacking and in the school. The problem was that, although she went calmly into canter the first time she was asked, and was well-balanced for her age, once she had returned to trot again the trot became short, choppy and hollow, and when she was asked for canter again she was tense and came above the bit. The rider was frustrated and at her wits end. Should she do lots of canter transitions and hope to make them boring and therefore not something to get worked up about? Or, since the first transition and canter were always calm, should she stick at just one canter episode in each schooling session?

This rider needed more information, because any approach she might decide on would have to rest on a theory about what was happening and why. So we started by simply describing the pattern. First time of asking – fine, either rein, balanced, rounded, calm. After this first canter, the mare became tense and hollow in trot, and the next canter transition was the same. Once actually into the second canter, she was balanced again. It seemed that she was anticipating, and that the antici-pation was causing the tension. Perhaps she could hardly wait, because she enjoyed the canter so much? However the pattern had originally begun, it was certainly now the case that the rider was anticipating problems with the trot and any following transitions, so the horse was likely to be sensing this – but without understanding it. And human emotion confuses horses, particularly young ones. They are trying to make sense of us – and indeed we are expecting them to – but how can you make sense of something which is powerful but which you don't understand? We made a list of more information the rider needed. What was the mare's early experience of being asked for canter? How was she being asked now? Was she being prepared enough – or too much? What were the patterns of the rider's schooling sessions?

Because we tend to repeat work on both reins, most horses learn to expect that canter right pretty soon follows canter left. A forward-going horse who enjoys cantering is likely to want to do more. What would happen if the rider immediately asked for canter again? Or if she persisted with the ten minutes of choppy trot she seemed to get after one canter and sat it out until the horse realized there wasn't going to be a second canter just yet? Was the mare different on the lunge?

There are no 'right' answers – but there were questions the rider could usefully ask herself, and things she could do systematically rather than randomly to get useful answers.

This rider had plenty of experience both of riding and of bringing on young horses. But what helped her most was not being given a 'how-to' recipe, but being asked to pay attention to the messages she was giving her horse, both intentionally and unintentionally, and to take second position with the young mare. In our wish to find solutions, we often forget to examine how the problem is being structured and repeated. This brings us back to the NLP axiom that reminds us 'If you always do what you've always done, you'll always get what you've always got'. So if you want change, you have to make a change. And there's another axiom that reminds us that the meaning of any communication is what the receiver understands by it – which may not be the same as what we intended!

TIP If you have a repeating pattern, describe it in detail, getting as full a sequence as you can. Experiment with changing it, starting with the simplest and easiest change you can make. Change only one thing at a time, and note what happens. Then you have experimental control and know what's causing what.

From his coaching experience, Timothy Gallwey identified three useful criteria for selecting what kinds of things to observe. What you should concentrate on needs to be: *observable, relevant and interesting.*

Observable means something that can be verified: something that you see, hear or feel kinesthetically, or something that you know you think or feel emotionally. Something observable, by and large, answers the questions 'What?', 'When?', 'Where?', 'How?', 'Who?' but not the question 'Why?' Since, when we do something, we don't always think consciously about why we're doing it, being asked 'Why?' afterwards can often make us rationalize or, worse, induce defensiveness – even if we're the one asking ourselves. This is not to say that rationalization, or finding reasons, is necessarily a negative process. It is, in fact, essential – in the right context. However, reasons tend to be theoretical, and theories are not the same as, or substitutes for, evidence. The value of the 'What?', 'When?', 'Where?', 'How?' questions is that they direct us towards evidence – something that we can notice, use, or change.

Relevant implies something that is part of or affects what you're trying to observe. NLP coaching encourages us to recognize that many things are relevant to riding: feelings, beliefs, attitudes, states of mind all have an impact – even on the technical aspects of riding – because so much of the material we're working with is us!

Interesting. Developing your observational skills calls for commitment and effort. What's going to make that worth while? Improving, certainly; but the best way of ensuring that you make that commitment and give that effort is that the process itself is interesting to you, moment by moment, as you do it. In coaching, there's a concept of developing and working with **flow**, which this idea relates to. Flow is what comes naturally, easily, fluently. Usually, flow means we're at one with ourselves and whatever we're doing. It's not necessarily about high levels of skill, but rather about a feeling of appropriateness, absorption and harmony within ourselves. Doing something we're really interested in contributes greatly to a sense of flow.

Basically, we're more inclined to do things which grab our attention than we are to do things which don't, but which we 'ought' to do. In Chapter 8 I'm going to take this even further, and explain how the best, and most productive, state for improving riding I know of is a state of play. If you want to follow this idea up now, go straight to that chapter. Reading a book is something else which often seems to have built-in 'oughts' about it – but many books address certain issues which may be of special significance to individual readers. Therefore, reading a book in the order in which it most urgently engages and informs you may be the most constructive use of that book from your personal perspective.

Calibration – Spotting Differences and Changes

NLP uses the word calibration to label the process of noticing and measuring changes. This observational tool is highly relevant to anyone engaged in learning and practising a skill. When your teacher comments that your horse has lost engagement through a corner, or that he's coming above the bit, she's calibrating changes in his behaviour from one moment to another. The picture she has in her mind at that moment has changed from the picture of a moment ago. And when she sets out to give you a lesson, or talks about what you and your horse might achieve in the next six months, she's calibrating again – measuring the difference between what she registers now and what she hopes or intends you'll be achieving at those points in the future.

Calibration isn't the prerogative of the highly qualified. We all learnt to calibrate from the moment we first saw how our mother or father's face changed as a result of something we did. It might have been the first indication of a big smile, or the frown that then led to a telling-off. Perhaps even earlier, we calibrated differences in our own experience between comfort and discomfort. Something had changed. These are examples of unconscious calibration. But we can also calibrate consciously. Planning where to hang a picture, and adjusting it for straightness once it's hung, are examples of conscious calibration. And there's another difference, too – once you've learnt how to calibrate something, and have done it many times, you begin to do it automatically. If, at present, it feels strange and over-deliberate to be calibrating consciously the difference in your horse's forwardness, or softness over the back, during a schooling session, remind yourself that the more you do it the easier it will become. As with reading, a complex process can soon become so automatic that you will be concerned only with its results, not how you achieved them.

> **I** REMEMBER WHEN I first watched Arthur Kottas, the First Chief Rider of the Spanish Riding School, taking a clinic I found it quite frustrating. He would just call out to the riders things like: 'More through', or 'More on the bit'. At that stage in my learning I wanted to be told *how* to get the horse more through, or onto the bit at all. But the experienced riders I was watching needed only to told what their trainer wanted, not how to achieve it. They already knew, and because they knew they could automatically do what was needed. They could use his comment to calibrate the changes they needed to make.

Calibration involves measuring the difference between two items. You can use different models – other people, past experiences, your visions of the future – as one of the points you need for calibrating. The other point is what's happening for you right now. Here are some examples to guide you:

1. Comparing what you're observing with how someone you admire does it. What are the similarities and differences? What's the difference that makes

the difference? What's the simplest change you can make to improve what you do?

2. Comparing how it feels now with how it feels when you get it right. What's different?

3. Remembering an outstanding moment or achievement. For example, the best trot he ever gave you. What exactly made that trot so special? Ride for it now.

4. Imagine as vividly as you can how you want it to be in the future. Involve information from as many senses as possible. Just how will it look? Just how will it feel? Hear the sounds of that rhythm of movement. Create what NLP calls a **compelling future** – a representation of what you want that is so strong and attractive that it positively draws you towards achieving it.

'The best trot he ever gave you...'
– Marisian and Charlie.

CHARLES DE KUNFFY uses a complex system of visual calibration to relate the pupil in front of him to several future points simultaneously, including how they'll look at the end of the lesson and in six months time. He relates all these points to his stored internal images of 'how the great riders do it'. One other trainer I know calibrates kinesthetically. The process is similar, but when she rides a horse she rides it from how it feels now to how she knows she wants it to feel in the future.

'From how it feels now to how she knows she wants it to be.'
Marisian and Feargus.

Skill-building Tips

- To start with, pay attention to one thing at a time. Make a deliberate choice about what you're going to attend to today, and perhaps for the next week or two. Don't put yourself under pressure – allow sufficient time until calibrating this point becomes automatic. Then pick something else to attend to. Or work on the two items alternately to give variety, but build up gradually.

- Start by concentrating on information from one of your senses. Then ask yourself what your other senses have to tell you about the same process or event. Make your internal understanding as rich as you can by drawing on every kind of sensory information – including taste and smell, if you can.

- Try an unfamiliar way of noticing things. If, like many riders, you rely heavily on sight, get someone to lunge you so that you can close your eyes and really notice the information you're getting kinesthetically. What's your seat telling you? How about the rhythm? If you can get the school to yourself, be bold and ride large, or ride circles with your eyes closed – the horse can't go anywhere. How much information can you gather like this? How do your feelings, and your posture, change when you open your eyes? How does the horse change when you close them? (He will!)

- Look for patterns. We ourselves and our horses are both creatures of habit. Repeating patterns can be used to duplicate successful experiences. On the other hand, patterns that seem to be problematic can be deconstructed once you know what's involved.

- Look out for the moment when something changes. Replay mentally what happened and ask yourself what was going on just before the moment of change. How did the change relate to what preceded it? Was there a gradual build-up, or a sudden stimulus?

- Calibrate your own experience and that of others. Watch friends doing their schooling. Go to competitions and watch a number of riders doing the same test. Calibrate the differences. Attend training clinics. Calibrate in your head how the riders on the clinic act – and then calibrate the similarities and differences between what you noticed and what the person taking the clinic noticed.

Becoming a keen detective of your own experiences is a great way to get the information you need to coach yourself. It's also fascinating, and because it involves you in detailed investigation it makes it difficult for you to be self-critical at the same time. Often, it's as if you are taking third position to observe what's going on, yourself included – and so there's no room for blame, or even praise. This doesn't mean that you are avoiding making judgements – in fact, the opposite, for calibration is entirely a matter of judgement. However, the kind of judgements you're *not* making when you're in inquiry mode are those black-and-white ones which involve your emotions and get you feeling pressurized to maintain achievement, or despairing because you haven't. Whether we're seeking to help ourselves or others, we need judgements that open up possibilities and give us even more information, not ones that close down the search.

In this chapter I've explored how one kind of comparative process can help us as riders. In the next one I'm going to show you how adding a third point of reference can help us even further. This is a tool with an application to self-coaching that I've developed especially for this book. It's called **triangulation**.

4

Triangulation

TRIANGULATION OFFERS US the key to knowing where we are and moving on. The idea of triangulation comes from map reading. Imagine yourself standing in a landscape:

Even as you look at this diagram, you will be noticing where X is in relation to the brackets that form the corners of the imagined landscape. One way to describe the position of X is to say that it is lower than, and to the left of, an imagined centre. Another way to describe the position of X is to say that it's closer to the left-hand vertical boundary and further from the right. It's also closer to the lower boundary and further from the top one. All these are ways of helping you to locate a position – and each involves plotting X in relation to other things (the imagined centre, the external boundaries).

It's the same if you want to know where you are in a landscape. You need to relate yourself to two other points of reference. This enables you to find out where you stand. One reference point might be a hill, another a valley, or one might be a coastline, another a church. To pinpoint your position you're using information like closeness and the angle or direction. Once you know where you are at present in relation to the landmarks around you, you can work out what you need to do in order to get where you want to go. You can plan your journey, and work out from the changing distances and angles between you and your chosen landmarks whether you're going in the right direction and how far you've gone.

So how can orientation skills, originally rooted in map reading and landscape, help you as a rider? When I was asking other riders about their problems and strategies for managing solo schooling, I had a really interesting conversation with my friend Nikki, whose experiences form one of the case-studies at the end of this book. It became clear as we talked that, in order to judge problems and progress, we often had to involve three things. If we only had two, such as how things were now and how we wanted them to be, we could only look at the differences between them. Of course that's useful, up to a point. In NLP, two-point comparison can take the form of contrastive analysis (how are things different, how are they the same?) and calibration (how have things changed?). However, once you start asking which difference makes the real difference you are into a three-point analysis, and that gives you much more information and a basis for measuring and evaluating the action you choose to take, because it allows for movement. This is triangulation, the concept that leapt into my mind as Nikki and I looked at the pattern of our discussion and tried to work out what kind of processing we were doing and how it could help other riders.

YOU MIGHT BE SEARCHING, for example, for what NLP calls 'the difference that makes the difference'. To do this, you have to hold three points in your mind and examine the relationship between them. Let's suppose that your horse isn't going forward. Point one is how things are right now. Point two is how you'd like him to be. Your point three comes in once you start considering whether your horse isn't going forward *because* he's tired from a heavy schooling session the day before, or *because* you aren't asking him clearly enough. You are now relating your first two items to a third.)

The example I've given shows you how triangulating can help plot what might cause or maintain a problem (in this case, lack of forwardness), and can also help you to assess the relative effectiveness of any changes you make.

How Triangulation Works

The great thing about triangulation is that it gives us a clear structure to work with. Let's see what kinds of situations it can help us with.

1. Working out where you are now in relation to your aims.

Point one: how things are now – for example, your horse is often above the bit.

Point two: how you want things to be – for example, you want him on the bit all the time.

Point three: the difference between one and two, as indicated by things like your self-assessment, your trainer's comments or your theoretical understanding. For example, you have read that, in order to be on the bit, the horse needs to raise his back – and your trainer says he is hollow much of the time, especially in trot.

Possible courses of action: get your trainer or a friend to tell you if the horse is less hollow when you are in rising trot than when you are in sitting trot, or help you to learn how to bring his back up under you more.

2. Working out the difference that makes a difference.

Point one: an experience that went well – examples • a smooth, forward, balanced downward transition • a dressage test that got a high mark.

Point two: a similar experience that went less well, or badly – examples • an abrupt or unbalanced downward transition • the same test on another day that got a lower mark.

Point three: the differences between one and two. • In the first example, when you achieved a good downward transition, you prepared the horse with a half-halt which helped him engage and balance into the transition more. • In the second example, on one occasion your horse went to the show alone and was quite calm, whereas on the other occasion he went in the same lorry as his friend and was then distracted by his friend whinnying from the lorry park.

Possible courses of action. Make a habit of preparing all downward transitions with a half-halt; practise your half-halts more; practise transitions more. • *Take your horse out on his own more; be firmer about demanding his attention when he's in the ring – even if it costs you marks and feels like schooling rather than competing.*

3. Assessing your progress towards your aims.

Point one: your aim – for example, you want to keep your feet correctly positioned in the stirrups all the time in canter.

Point two: how things used to be – for example, your feet always used to slip 'home' every time you cantered.

Point three: how far you have moved in the desired direction – for example, now they tend to slip home only when you are cantering on the right rein.

Possible courses of action: check what differences there are between the work on each rein, for example, are you sitting more to the left; are you bringing your right leg up and gripping; are you collapsing your right hip; do you need to step down more into your right stirrup; is your horse more supple and smooth on the left rein?

4. Comparing the effectiveness of different strategies.

Point one: the issue or problem – for example, you have been frightened of hacking since a nasty fall which occurred when your horse shied as a bird flew out suddenly in front of him.

Point two: the effect of strategy (a) – you made yourself go hacking, felt fearful all the time and communicated your anxiety to your horse.

Point three: the effect of strategy (b) – you stopped hacking altogether.

Course of action: if you have several possible strategies to evaluate, your next step is to compare whichever of (a) or (b) is better as against next possibility (c), then whichever of those is better with (d) and so on, each time comparing a new strategy with the best so far until you have found the very best. This process may sound laborious but it ensures you don't try to evaluate too much information at once and thus confuse your findings. In the example given, you may conclude that, while strategy (b) removed the anxiety, it means that you'll have to stay in the school, so you think (a) is better. However (c), which is going out with a sensible friend on her bomb-proof horse, seems better than (a). Then you consider strategy (d), which involves changing the disaster movies you are currently running in your head so that they incorporate an increased feeling of safety and control, which arises from the deeper and more secure seat you are developing through doing lots of trotting without stirrups, which means that you are much more likely to stay put. This solution seems best of all, but you decide to play safe and combine it with strategy (c), going out with your friend, as well.

5. Understanding how the same situation may be viewed by different participants or from different perspectives.

This form of triangulation involves using the concept of 'positions' described in Chapter 1, for example triangulating the views of yourself, your horse and your trainer; or yourself, your horse and a real or imagined observer; or yourself, your horse and your ideal.

Point one: your perspective (first position). You are feeling upset because your horse is fit and keeps barging through the bridle and you can't get him to do what you want.

Point two: your horse's perspective (second position). 'It's autumn and I'm having to stay in my box much more than I was a few weeks ago. I'm dying to stretch my legs like I did in the field and she keeps wanting to slow me down. I'm really frustrated.'

Point three: (third position) You and your horse have different outcomes in mind here! Neither of you is 'right' or 'wrong' – but you certainly need to find a way to harmonize.

Possible courses of action: you decide to put your horse into a good forward canter for a few circuits (or take him for a short hack) before schooling him; you loose-school him over small jumps before schooling under saddle; you lunge him to get the fizziness and the bucks out of him before you ride him.

These are some examples of the reference points you can triangulate to give you a current position and to help you forward. It's likely that you will be able to think of others.

The process of triangulation is both clear and flexible in itself. You can add further dimensions to its effectiveness in two ways, which I'm going to explain in more detail. The first is to gather more information by checking your full range of sensory systems rather than just drawing on your favourite (the one which comes most naturally to you). I call this a **sensory system check**. The second is to verify the results you get by checking their meaning and impact against certain criteria which have been identified by NLP as significant – a **logical level check**.

Sensory System Check

I explained earlier that when we think, we do so in different ways. We can all make use of our senses to replay or create thoughts in our minds: different people have their own favourite senses. We don't know why some people seem to be natural picture-makers, and others have a strong sense of physical experience (or sound, or smell, or taste) when they think of the same things, but they certainly do. This means that each of us will receive more information through our favoured system(s) and will process it internally by the same system(s) when we're thinking about the past or imagining the future. These representational system patterns, as NLP calls them, are our own thinking signatures. However, it is not simply the case that we favour a certain system or systems – we are also affected more strongly by certain aspects of it (or them) than others. For example, some people who favour visual systems find large, bright, coloured images powerful whereas small, washed out or black-and-white images are less powerful for them. For some people who favour kinesthetic systems, pressure is more influential than rhythm, or vice versa. These features are called **sub-modalities** in NLP because they are sub-divisions within the larger 'modality' of the particular representational system involved. You'll find a list of the most common sub-modalities in the Appendix at the end of this book, together with some ways to work out which are most influential for you.

When you're triangulating, it's helpful to check which representational systems and which sub-modalities are operating. To take the example of the downward transitions again: if you're primarily or strongly visual, are you watching yourself from outside as you make the transition – or are you looking out of your own eyes? How much detail is there? Is the picture static or moving? What happens if you change one of these sub-modalities? If you're looking at the situation from inside, what happens if you step outside yourself and imagine you're watching it on film? For many people, this particular change distances them from the emotion and makes it easier to evaluate or analyse what's going on. On the other hand, if you're viewing a good experience with this distanced perspective, you may get more enjoyment and pride out of it if you 'step inside' and let yourself feel just how good it is.

Or perhaps you're seeing the 'good' transition you want as small, blurred and distant, and the 'bad' one as all too close and sharp. What happens if you bring the good one closer and sharpen the detail? Do you notice more of how that transition comes about? Do you feel you own it more? If the picture is still, what happens if you turn it into a movie?

There's no right and wrong about these variations – the objective is to find out how you do things, so you can do more of what works and less of what doesn't. If the images are moving and scary, it can help to freeze-frame them or turn them into snapshots. Enjoyable experiences, by contrast, may become even better if you allow them to flow.

You may also find that deliberately adding more information from one of your less-favoured representational systems helps you. For example, if your favoured system is visual, try adding in the kinesthetic. First 'watch' a well-prepared transition, then add in the feeling of how your weight shifts back and down, and how your horse's pelvis tucks under as he steps into the transition. If you haven't noticed this feeling before, imagine how it would feel. To help yourself, access how it feels by tucking your own pelvis under you now, as you sit on the chair reading this, or bring yourself to a halt from walking around your home or down the street and notice what happens as you do so. This rebalancing and 'sitting' is what you need to do yourself in order to help your horse to do the same.

When we take information from more than one sensory system, we enrich the representation and make it more powerful. When we're triangulating, checking for information from our less-favoured senses gives us more to work with, and thus more leverage in improving or changing things. In fact, it may be that the key factor in change lies in one of your less-favoured systems. For example, you might be running a fearful picture of falling off over a larger fence than you're used to but, when you investigate, you find that the thing that's really stopping you is a half-remembered experience from childhood when your aunt, who was watching you ride, said: 'Aren't you frightened of jumping those big fences?' This auditory input has literally become a 'voice-over', which has been building and maintaining your fear.

Logical Level Check

One way of considering an experience is to ask yourself what kinds of issues are involved. NLP has identified a number of levels by which an experience can be assessed, which relate to different kinds of meaning and impact. One way of representing these levels is in the form of a ladder or hierarchy, thus:

Identity   Issues about who or what you are.

Beliefs and Values   Issues about what you believe, or what's important to you.

Capability	Issues about what you know, or can do.
Behaviour	Issues about actions – what you do and how you do it.
Environment	Issues to do with external circumstances.

Alternatively, you can regard the levels as a set of concentric circles, with identity, the closest to you, in the centre and environment, the most external, at the outside.

Arranging the levels in either order may suggest that identity, the one at the top or the centre, is somehow the most important. But the concept of logical levels – like other concepts in NLP – isn't value-loaded. It simply helps us to identify what kinds of things are going on. Issues of environment can be very important in shaping or influencing things. Just think of how a horse may become miserable, tetchy or even violent if his teeth or his saddle are causing him pain. The problem is one of environment. Get a better-fitting saddle, have his teeth rasped, and he's once more the sweet, cooperative soul you thought you owned. In this example, the cause was environmental and the problem was one of behaviour.

When you are triangulating, it can be really useful to have the logical levels in mind. In fact, they might be incorporated as starting points. Returning to the example of the horse who isn't going forward as you want him to, you might ask yourself whether the problem is one of identity (he's not a forward-going horse), or of capability (I don't know how to use my legs effectively enough), or of environment (he's tired; he needs more oats now that I'm asking him to work harder).

However, it's not always the case that the solution to a problem occurs on the same level as its cause, or on the level upon which you experience it. For example, perhaps you don't use your legs strongly enough because you're afraid of hurting your horse, or you don't want others to think you are rough with him. This is a matter of your beliefs and values rather than one of your physical strength (capability) or behaviour. And so you'll need to find out more about what's involved on the relevant level, and make changes there, if you are to deliver the 'wake up' reminder he might need to get him attentive and off the leg.

Many of the problems that riders experience arise because they take difficulties as failure at an identity level. If you catch yourself saying 'I'm no good as a rider', this is what may well be happening. Rephrasing this as 'I didn't get what I wanted today' takes the sting out of what happened and relocates your problem onto the level of behaviour. Or perhaps you might think 'I can't ride half-pass correctly – yet', which is a matter of capability. Both of these changes may make major differences to how you feel, and turn something which initially felt like a major failure into something for which you could begin to find a solution.

So, when you're triangulating, you'll find the logical levels very useful to have in your trio of points. You can use them at the start, as I've shown in the example, to help define what kind of problem you're dealing with, and you can use them at the end as a way of helping you find the most fitting steps to take next. And, of course, there are times when you can use them both at the beginning and the end. And the more you use them, the more automatic refining your evaluations in this way will become.

To recap, when you find yourself noticing a difference between how things are and how you'd like them to be, remind yourself that you can't go anywhere on a map or in a landscape if you don't have two points of reference apart from yourself. Even if you walk in a straight line from A to B you need to know how far you've gone and how far you still have to go. And when you're seeking to improve a skill, triangulation gives you the means of moving from a static state (how things are is different from how I want them to be) to an active, progressive, flowing, purposeful one.

Summarizing the Process

Let's summarize the process.

Triangulation is a process for self-assessment

It's *action* is to map out where you are in relation to:

- where you're coming from

- what you want and how you're going to get there

- how far you've got.

It *relates* three points from various options, such as:

- self (first-person perception)

- other (second-person perception)

to:

- how you were/used to be

- how you want to be (outcomes)

- models of excellence

- theoretical understanding.

It's *amplified and enriched* by a sensory system check.

It's *verified* by a logical level check.

And it *results in options* for action and change at all levels.

Triangulating is your first powerful tool for change.

Triangulation in Action – Working with Nikki G

I asked Nikki what she wanted to work on, not just in our session of that day but over the two months of our case-study work together. Nikki picked three items:

- *Further work on making her hands more level and equal (we had begun this work earlier in the year.)*

- *Helping her lower leg to come back further underneath her and stay there.*

- *Maintaining an upright posture, in order to enhance the effectiveness and feel of her seat.*

Rather than dive straight into working on these, I asked what larger aim improving in these ways would serve for her. She said 'I want my horse to be moving like a horse, and to be travelling forward under me'.

My question had helped Nikki to consider the detailed and specific positional aims she had started with in the context of the much larger purposes they were ultimately going to serve. By looking at her immediate aims in this

The starting point of the session: active but uninspired. Beamish is flat and not 'through', and Nikki is collapsing into a 'chair seat'. (Compare with photo on page 63.)

way, she could make sure that they were in line with her bigger goals – but she could also begin to consider other steps towards achieving the same goals. As a result, she could check out the relevance of her immediate targets and, at the same time, become open to other possible avenues of approach.

In NLP, this process of moving from smaller to larger – or larger to smaller – groupings within the same body of information is known as **chunking**. The concept is that you can cut the cake into larger or smaller chunks, but it is still the same cake. Another analogy might be that of a zoom lens on a camera: it views the same subject, but from closer or further and with more or less detail and more or less background. Different people will naturally tend to be comfortable working with certain chunk sizes (more of this in the next chapter); but really effective people in any sphere will have flexibility in moving in either direction.

Returning to Nikki's situation, she and I now had the three points for our triangulation.

Point one: Nikki's current riding style.

Point two: her style with the added positional improvements she wanted.

Point three: the larger goals which the improvements were intended to serve.

This choice revealed Nikki's belief (which I shared) that the improvements to her style would enable her horse, Beamish, to become more truly himself ('like a horse') in his ability to offer the best he could, and to go forward in better balance and self-carriage ('travelling under me').

At this point it would have been quite natural and easy to frame our coaching around the positional improvements Nikki wanted, using our NLP concepts and skills to take the process forward. But something made me use Nikki's own words to ask her, instead, to ride her warm-up with her larger goals, not her specific corrections in mind: 'Ride him towards being a horse and travelling forward under you'. Thinking about this now, I'd say that I instinctively kept Nikki to focused on her larger goals (bigger chunk) in order to open up still more possible avenues to achieving them.

With this larger purpose in his rider's mind, Beamish began to offer a relaxed and active walk with a good seven inch overtrack (I measured it). At this point, we added a sensory check. I asked Nikki what told her that Beamish was 'travelling' as she wanted in the walk, and she replied that it was the feeling of his back moving under her.

Next, they went on to produce a free, powerful and rhythmical trot. At this point, Beamish was in a long outline, and Nikki and I agreed that we would allow and expect him to bring himself into a shorter, more 'uphill' frame in his own time and of his own accord once he was freer and fully warmed up – as indeed he did about ten minutes later, without being asked.

Nikki and I were both very pleased with what was happening, and she proceeded from rising into sitting trot. I then noticed that, although she had been very upright and forward-looking in walk and rising trot, once sitting she tended to look down and to tilt slightly forward again. She also switched to working without stirrups, and this made her lower leg come forward, becoming more passive and less toned. I 'sculpted' her lower leg into the correct position (1) and asked her what differences she noticed between the two (contrastive analysis). Nikki said that she had recently been working to tone her thigh muscles, but now felt that they were becoming tight instead of toned, with the effect of actually blocking activity in the lower leg. As she demonstrated the toned position she had been aiming for, I could see how the lower

thigh muscle tightened and the upper one shortened, bringing her lower leg forward.

This told us what was happening, and perhaps why. More importantly, as it turned out, I saw that, as her leg came up, the angle at the top of her thigh became more acute (2).

I asked what had to happen in order for it to become more open, and Nikki replied that there needed to be more stretch over the front of the joint (3).

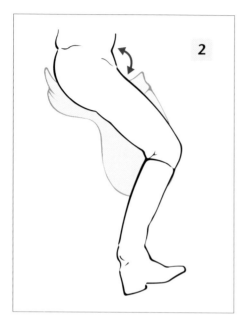

I then asked her to ride around feeling for that stretch. Immediately, her thigh became more vertical and her lower leg resumed a more correct position. And, interestingly, Beamish began to open up too, going more freely forward and coming up through the shoulder.

The stretch and lengthening Nikki made through the front of her thighs lifted and opened up her whole position and was immediately reflected in Beamish's ability to use himself more fully and expressively. Our session finished with a truly flying medium trot.

Often in riding, it seems that all we need to do is to work from how it is now towards how it ought to be – two points of reference. This session demonstrated clearly that, by triangulating those two points at the start with a third – the greater purpose Nikki had in mind – we bypassed a 'trying' mode and gained access to information that had not been previously available to either of us. While Beamish and Nikki both worked hard physically, they remained relaxed mentally.

Through chunking up, we began to triangulate differently. As the session progressed we shifted the base of our work to a different triangle, thus:

Point one: how it is now.

Point two: the greater purpose.

Point three: how do a series of experimental changes help movement from one to two?

If we look at this working session in terms of the logical levels, we can see that Nikki's original 'want-to' was in terms of her **capability** to produce a 'better' behaviour. Asking the wider purpose question took her up to the level of **beliefs and values**, where we worked to help Nikki's horse become more truly himself (thus, her **beliefs and values** concerning his **identity**), rather than limiting our focus and intention to the improvement of her technical capability. This meant that, when we did examine technicalities, it was with a view to how they served that greater purpose. This gave them a more profound and worthwhile meaning, and also dovetailed with Nikki's desire to become as good a rider as possible – an aim at a higher level still, that of her **identity**.

By chunking up in this way, we were able to align our work across the logical levels, ensuring a coherence of activity, purpose and achievement. Of course, analysing rapid events in this way can make them sound complex – and they are! Fortunately, it's enough for you when you're actually riding, planning your ride or thinking about it afterwards, to bear in mind the usefulness of looking at things with a different-sized filter from the one you naturally prefer, and to make this one of the triangulation points you work with. I might, for example, have made exactly the same points about a session in which a rider began with a large chunk size ('I want my horse to be expressively and fluently

Triangulation in action – 'expressively and fluently himself'. Nikki and Beamish at the end of the session.

himself') and needed helping to 'translate' this into the smaller chunks involved in deciding what specific behaviours would demonstrate that the horse was doing this, and what rider activities and schooling patterns would best help him.

Chunking Up

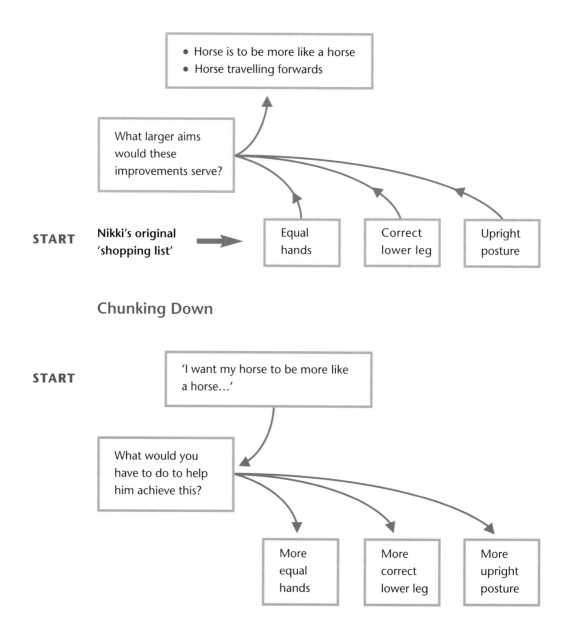

Chunking Down

5

Designing Your Motivation

ONE OF THE THINGS THAT makes riding unique is that you've got two living beings to work with: yourself and your horse. This means that, as a solo schooler, you have two 'clients' to coach. In this chapter and the next I'm going to outline further an NLP concept which is the ideal tool for helping you do this: it's the concept of **meta-programmes**, which I mentioned briefly in Chapter 2.

Everyone is different, in their attitudes, their abilities, their personalities and, as NLP has shown us, in the way they process information. Good teachers, managers, partners, parents and friends all know this and work with it, whether instinctively or deliberately. Successful people in any sphere are able to use this kind of understanding not only to get the most from others, but also to get the most from themselves. What NLP has been able to demonstrate is that, underlying the almost infinite variations between you and me and every-one else out there, are some patterns we do have in common, even though we combine them in different ways.

These are the meta-programmes – so called because they are patterns of thought and behaviour (programmes) which operate at a very high (meta) level of organisation, rather like the operating systems on computers as opposed to their individual software. Another analogy is that, just as a dimmer-switch allows us to set lighting at many different levels within two possible extremes, so a meta-programme describes a whole range of possibilities along a single axis between one extreme and another. As an example, we can refer once more to the difference between the optimist and the pessimist:

Person sees bottle containing liquid

X ——————————————————————————— Y

Optimist   **Pessimist**
thinks it's half-full   thinks it's half-empty

The information they are each dealing with is the same, but the way in which they interpret it is different, because they have different underlying attitudes and assumptions.

Quite a number of meta-programmes, which all have to do with the ways we process information, have been identified and described. Among them are some that are really useful for us as riders and, in this chapter, I'm going to explore a few key ones which can help us to coach ourselves and train our horses

The first point to understand is that your personal, natural way of thinking or behaving could be anywhere along the line between one meta-programme extreme and the other. There's no better or worse, right or wrong, place for you to be operating from – except in relation to the situation you're in and the results you want. It's the fit that matters. Knowing where you stand allows you to recognize the strengths and weaknesses of your position – and to make changes if you want to.

I'm going to give you a brief profile of each extreme of these key meta-programmes, and some examples of the strengths and weaknesses inherent in those extremes. Of course, few people are truly 'either/or' but, as you read, you'll be able to plot which extreme you are closer to on each meta-programme, and see its advantages and disadvantages for your riding. You'll also discover something about how other people operate – and why, perhaps, you find it easy to get along with them or, alternatively, don't 'see eye to eye'. I'm also going to show you how you can harness your natural ways of thinking to help motivate yourself, and how you can develop your flexibility through some exercises that stretch you into your less familiar ways of operating.

Let's start with the meta-programme I worked with in Nikki's lesson (Triangulation in Action).

Preferred Chunk Size

Small Chunk ———————————————————— Large Chunk

Small Chunk

We all know some people whose preference is for small chunk size: they are the ones who are good with detail.

Small chunk pluses
A small chunk person may be precise and accurate, in what they do, in what they notice, in what they remember, in what they're interested in.

Small chunk pitfalls
They may also 'fail to see the wood for the trees', because they 'get lost in the detail' or are 'too close up to get the big picture'.

Large Chunk

People with this preference, on the other hand, see the picture as a whole.

Large chunk pluses
They have the grand visions, the wonderful goals. They 'get the idea'.

Large chunk pitfalls
Sometimes these grand ideas won't be grounded in here-and-now realities, or the person may have difficulty in working out exactly what they need to do to achieve them. Large chunk people may be impatient with detail – particularly if it doesn't seem to fit in with their grand plan.

There can also be another tendency that's sometimes associated with smaller/larger chunk size processing – the tendency for small chunk people to be more focused on here and now and the tendency of large chunk people to be more focused on the future.

Chunking Language

You may already have recognized where you tend to come on this particular meta-programme axis. Language is one of the great give-aways: if you listen, to yourself and to others, you'll pick up clues which begin to build the profile for you.

Small chunk phrases		*Large chunk phrases*	
detail	scrutinize	global	big picture
'how-tos'	examine	larger view	in the main
specific	fill in	overall	expand
precisely/exactly		vision	

Motivation

Tips for motivating yourself if you prefer small chunks. Think about:

• What exactly is involved in this?

• What precisely do I need to do?

• Describe... identify...

• What comes first...?

• What specific steps are involved in the process?

Tips for motivating yourself if you naturally prefer large chunks. Ask yourself:

• What's my riding goal – what will it look like, feel like, sound like?

• What's the effect I want to achieve?

• What impact would doing x have on achieving my goal?

• What's the ultimate vision I have for my horse and myself?

Stretching Yourself

Tips for stretching yourself if you prefer small chunks. Guideline – build up the puzzle:

• Think about small steps – start where you are then build up towards the bigger picture/overall goal.

• Ask yourself how the pieces fit together.

• Start with 'now' – work towards 'then'.

• Think about what comes first – then what's next – then after that...?

• Ask yourself 'Where does this lead to?'

• How does it/could it contribute to something bigger/better?

• If I go on doing this, where will it get me?

Tips for stretching yourself if you prefer large chunks. Guideline – find out how it's all put together:

• What are the building blocks?

• What can you do today – and how will it fit into your bigger aim?

• Work backwards from your goal, chunking it down into do-able, achievable steps.

1. Goal

2. What would that involve?

3. What would that involve?

4. What would that involve?

...Take as many steps as you need until you finally get to:

What do I need to do today?

You now have a sequence of specific steps which you can use to guide your actions from 'Today' through to 'Goal'.

RIDER PROFILES

Small Chunk

Lizzie thinks of herself as a 'slow learner' – but actually she just likes to do one thing at a time. She's meticulous and well-organized, and she likes to get each step right before she builds on it. The first time she tried a half-pass she just 'couldn't get her head around it'. But when her trainer broke it down into steps and asked her to practise each step before adding the next, she found it really easy. 'It's simple,' she said. 'First you get the horse straight. Then you point his nose and shoulder across on a diagonal so that he's bent around your inside leg. Then you just put your outside leg back and bring his quarters with you.'

Frankie is also a small-chunker. Her friends at the yard sometimes find her a bit irritating because she seems to give equal importance to everything, rather than prioritizing. She doesn't seem able to cut corners – even ordinary ones – and things take her longer to learn and to do because she focuses on such small things. Even Frankie is beginning to wonder if there isn't a way to simplify life.

Large Chunk

Sam was a natural rider, with a bold approach across country. He had a number of local successes, and his friends encouraged him to enter for his first one-day event. He thought he'd give it a go, and imagined himself having a great day and perhaps even getting placed. But though he and his horse both enjoyed showjumping and could just about manage a simple dressage test, what Sam had forgotten was that doing all three disciplines on one day requires fitness and stamina. Neither he nor his horse was fit enough, so they ended up having three refusals across-country. Sam realized that, in future, he would need a longer and much more systematic build-up – even before just 'having a go'.

Bella is also a person who has grand visions. They are what inspire her and what keep her going when times are tough. She always wanted to breed and bring on a horse of her own, and she knew that, one day, she would win a showing championship with her own youngster. From her earliest riding school days this was what she was aiming for and, over the years, she equipped herself with the skills and experience she needed – and eventually bred a promising youngster from a friend's mare who had been an insurance write-off after injury. Now the youngster has already had some successes, and Bella is pretty sure she's on track for her grand vision.

Direction of Motivation

Moving Towards ————————————————— Moving Away From

Moving Towards

Some people are motivated by new ideas, aims, possibilities. They seek excitement and challenge. They like what's different. The future can be their magnet. This is a **towards** motivation.

'Towards' pluses
These people are happy to experiment. They are not afraid of taking risks. They relish the challenge of something different and enjoy working in their stretch zone. They 'respond to the carrot'.

'Towards' pitfalls
They may take on too much, too soon. They may leave things incomplete, or not see them through – they 'may not deliver'. They may chop and change and can be taken in by the latest fad.

Moving Away From

Other people are motivated to move **away from** situations, to improve things they don't like or that aren't right, or to avoid situations that they don't think they can improve. Whereas 'towards' people are instinctively attracted to change and innovation, 'away from' people are driven to change by discomfort and dissatisfaction. They 'respond to the stick'.

'Away from' pluses
They are spurred on to make changes by something that doesn't work. They tend to complete, to finalize. They generally comply with expectations and requirements (including rules and regulations). They are motivated to get out of trouble.

'Away from' pitfalls
They can be so busy looking over their shoulder that they aren't looking where they're going. They are reactive not proactive. They may feel driven rather than being in charge.

Directional Motivation Language

'Towards' phrases	*'Away from' phrases*
Why not?	What if…?
Give it a go	Supposing…
Let's try it on for size	I'd better…
Better	Let's make sure
I like the idea of…	It's not working

Motivation

Tips for motivating yourself if you are a 'towards' person:

• Imagine how you will feel when/how it will be when…

• Imagine the benefits.

• What will you learn by doing this?

• What will you gain by doing this?

Tips for motivating yourself if you are an 'away from' person:

• What will happen if you don't…?

• What do you dislike about the current situation?

• What irritates/disappoints you about how things are?

• What's going wrong?

Stretching Yourself

Tips for stretching yourself if you are a 'towards' person. Guideline – take out insurance:

• What needs doing before you try out x?

• What contributes towards achieving x?

• Do you have the pieces in place already?

- If not, what do you need to do next in order to move on?

- What might be the pitfalls of x? Or its disadvantages?

Tips for stretching yourself if you are an 'away from' person. Guideline – also look for the bright side:

- Imagine how it will be when you've solved this problem.

- What's the best thing about how things are right now?

- What's the first benefit you'll notice when...?

- What's the positive side of this experience?

RIDER PROFILES

Towards

Susie and her Arab gelding Shazam really enjoyed doing a bit of everything. They jumped a bit, hacked a bit, showed a bit, did a bit of dressage. When Susie's friend Chris said that he was organizing a sponsored ride to raise money for charity, he asked Susie if she'd help out by signing up. Susie went round her office getting sponsors – 'I'm doing it for a bit of a laugh and because it's for a good cause', she said. 'I bet we'll come home last.' They had some hairy moments, and avoided the biggest jumps; but all in all they had a great day – and came home about 20th, which thrilled Susie to bits. 'I think I might have a go at a proper long distance ride now', she said.

Tom was also a 'towards' person, game for anything. He started riding in his early thirties to keep his children company, and really enjoyed it. After he'd been riding for about a year, a friend offered him a retired hunter on loan. 'What a good idea', Tom thought, 'It will be great to have a horse of my own, rather than just going to a riding school. I'll be able to go hacking on my own, and do a bit of jumping'. So he took up the offer and arranged livery at the riding stables. But it wasn't long before he found that having his own horse was very different from just turning up for rides twice a week. He didn't have time to ride every day, and began to feel that the horse was more of a burden, requiring planning and organization, than the delight he'd anticipated. The horse was quite elderly, and rather stiff, so he really needed riding more often than Tom could manage. Also, he had been used to a more experienced rider, and Tom had some alarming experiences when he rode out alone. After a few months Tom had to admit that he'd taken on more than he could manage. 'That's me all over', he said. 'I leap before I look.'

Away From

Rachel took up dressage in her thirties, and really wanted to do well. Since she had a well-paid job she could afford lessons – in fact, she booked two a week because she hated looking like a beginner. Rachel had good balance and gentle hands, and she was prepared to put time into practising what she was taught, so she and her horse Toby began to make good progress. But Rachel found it really difficult to take on board the praise her teacher was giving her – she just kept on watching videos and reading books and thinking how much less good she was than the experts she admired. One day she was in despair after a lesson. 'Toby just wasn't going forward enough', she told a friend at the yard.

'But I heard your teacher say how soft and obedient he was, and how rhythmical', her friend said. 'You can't have been listening. If you go on believing that you're not good enough, even when you're being told you're actually doing quite well, you might as well give up right now! Or you could open up your ears and take heart'.

'I just find it difficult to believe that anything I do is good enough', Rachel agreed.

Lucy was an 'away from' processor, too. She was always aware of how dangerous a sport riding could be, and how unpredictable horses were – even the nicest of them. But she loved riding, and her caution helped her to make safe and sensible decisions. She imagined what might go wrong and used it to keep safe – but she didn't frighten herself with disaster scenarios. If she wasn't sure of anything, she took time to think it through. She avoided unnecessary risks, kept a careful eye out for potential dangers and enjoyed her riding all the more because of it.

Method of Approach

Prefers Options ———————————————— Prefers Procedures

Options

Some people like choice, variety, difference. They like exercising choice for its own sake. They enjoy experimentation. They are often impatient with rules and regulations, which they may feel are stuffy or constricting. They may want to bend the rules. These are **options** people.

Options pluses

These people are good at improvising and are not phased by having to make decisions. They can be creative and innovative, either imaginatively or practically. They probably enjoy, and are good at, solving problems.

Options pitfalls

They may become restless with routine. They may chop and change and want to cut corners. They may not spend enough time on the basics because they find them boring.

Procedures

Other people like to know how to go about things. They understand how complex processes are sequenced. They feel safe doing things in order. They respect rules and regulations. They are comfortable with being told how to go about something. For them, 'ought' is a good word. They don't like to cut corners, and may shy away from experimentation. These are **procedures** people.

Procedures pluses

They can be patient and meticulous and make good trainers – provided things go according to plan. Where something can be built up by careful repetition, they'll stick at it. They are reliable.

Procedures pitfalls

They may be rigid and rule-bound, and stick at something for too long when it isn't working because 'it ought to work' or 'it's just done like that'. They may become flustered or anxious when faced with a situation that falls outside the rules.

Methodology Language

Options phrases
What else?
How else?
Decide
Choose
What are the options...?
Alternatives

Procedures phrases
The right way
In order
That's how it's done
The Rulebook says...
Tried and tested
Established...

Motivation

Tips for motivating yourself if you are an 'options' person:

- Think of different ways to achieve something.

- Think of several solutions to a problem.

- Play with alternative possibilities.

Tips for motivating yourself if you are a 'procedures' person:

- Model others who do something well that you'd like to do better – find out exactly how they do it – copy them.

- Identify the sequences involved in working towards your aim, in learning a skill, and follow them in order.

- Keep records and notes to refer back to and to help you with future planning.

Stretching Yourself

Tips for stretching yourself if you are an 'options' person. Guideline – load for success by choosing between procedures that are already known to work:

- How many different ways have been developed for approaching this problem/goal? What can you learn from them?

- Practise evaluating and choosing between different ways of going about things – learn to appreciate a good procedure, not just a good result.

Tips for stretching yourself if you are a 'procedures' person. Guideline – open up the avenues:

- Once you've found a scheme/pattern/routine that works – ask about others.

- Try out a proven pattern that's new to you.

- Ask yourself 'What else?'

- Pretend that some key element in one of your usual patterns was missing. How would you manage without it? What else might you do instead? And what else beyond that?

- Generate a number of procedural options – and choose between them.

- How would you choose between two routines that both work? What hidden criteria are you using?

RIDER PROFILES

Options

Let's go back to Susie again, because she really illustrates both the strengths and the limitations of an options approach. Susie really enjoyed doing a bit of every-thing. She was game for trying a new discipline – or for riding a different horse – any time the chance came up. She tried a bit of Western riding, she went along with a friend who was into driving and hung out the back of the carriage as balance. One reason why she enjoyed her horse, Shazam, was the fact that he was quite an all-rounder, too. Sometimes she felt a little envious when friends at the yard came home with rosettes from the competitions they'd been to – but then she reminded herself that they had spent long hours just doing dressage, or prac-tising their jumping.

'I know I'd get bored spending all that time on just one thing', she said to herself. 'I guess I'll just have to go on being a jack-of-all-trades and master of none. That's how I seem to be, so I might as well enjoy it.' In fact, Susie had recog-nized what kind of person she was in this respect, knew the implications and was prepared to accept the 'trade-off' between the enjoyment her all-round approach gave her and the fact that she probably wouldn't get to a really high level in any single discipline. And that is one of the pay-offs of knowing your own meta-programme profile.

Procedures

Mike was a solicitor who enjoyed riding in his spare time. He had a large horse called Clara, and they both enjoyed jumping. Clara had a big jump, but she spent quite a lot of time in the air and wasn't fast enough for speed classes. However, Mike enjoyed the precision of riding a good round. As he walked the course beforehand, he liked to plan how he'd take the corners, how many strides he'd allow, when he'd ask Clara to take off. For him, planning and riding to plan was half the fun of it. He rode and competed regularly, and began to have some successes, gradually qualifying Clara for bigger shows and higher levels. Because of Clara's careful ability and big jump, and Mike's calm and accurate approach, Mike's trainer suggested that they should specialize in puissance. 'You're no good

---

for the speed classes', she said bluntly. 'You waste time and I can see from your face how much it pains you to hurry. Do what comes naturally.'

Grace was also a procedural person. She was keen to become a good rider, and took regular lessons from a respected trainer. She read the books and watched the videos, went to the lecture-demos and worked hard to emulate the riders whose skills and achievements she admired. Because she was the kind of person who always liked to do things 'by the book', she ran into a couple of problems with her riding. One was that sometimes the authorities she admired didn't agree – so whose view should she adopt? It was important to do things the right way – but whose way was that? The other problem she found was that, over time, she lost confidence in her own ability, even though (perhaps because) she tried so hard to do what her trainer taught her and what the books said she should be doing. She felt anxious and unsure when riding on her own – so she drifted into a pattern of schooling only when she had her trainer with her. Other days, she 'just hacked'. But this didn't help either, because as she became even more dependent on her trainer, she felt even less confident in her own ability. It seemed that she would never be able to 'get it right' on her own.

Source of Reference

Internal (self) ————————————————— External (other)

When we reach an opinion on some issue, or arrive at a judgement, we do so with reference to something. It's actually a form of triangulation, the three points being:

Thing being judged

Authority being referred to for the judgement – self or other

Opinion/judgement

Self-referenced

Some people naturally base their judgements on their own feelings, experiences and values. They are **self-referenced**.

Self-referenced pluses
These people can often be confident. They are not bothered by others' opinions. They know what they want and why they want it. They are often clear and decisive.

Self-referenced pitfalls
They may be opinionated or stubborn. They may ignore useful information or guidance because it comes from outside. They may be egotistical and find it difficult to imagine or understand the impact they have on others.

Other-referenced

Other people tend to look outside for support or verification. They may put other people's judgements before their own, or consider other people's feelings and needs as more important than their own. They are **other-referenced**.

Other-referenced pluses
They consider others' views and needs to be important – they are often considerate and likeable. They can easily step into second position and imagine how others will react.

Other-referenced pitfalls
They may be self-effacing to the point of allowing themselves to be trodden on. They can fall in with others and then find themselves being resentful. They often lack confidence in their own skills or judgements. They may find it hard to be decisive.

Self- and Other-referenced Language

Self-referenced
Statements beginning with I think, I feel, I want, etc.

Other-referenced
Statements beginning with He/she/the experts wants/needs/feels/says...

Motivation

Tips for motivating yourself if you are self-referenced:

• Clarify your own values and your opinions on things.

• Work from what you want and think.

Tips for motivating yourself if you are other-referenced:

• How would you like to come across (to your trainer, to your horse)?

• How do you think you are coming across at the moment?

• Could you make a better impression?

• What could you do to deserve a better opinion from them?

Stretching Yourself

Tips for stretching yourself if you are self-referenced. Guideline – take another perspective:

• Ask yourself what he/she may be thinking/feeling/wanting (i.e. take second position).

• Ask yourself, as if you were an observer, how you and your actions will be coming across (i.e. take third position).

• Ask yourself whether you want them to have that impression of you.

• Ask yourself how you can check out if that is, in fact, the impression you're giving.

Tips for stretching yourself if you are other-referenced. Guideline– put yourself in the picture:

• Step into third position, as if you were someone coaching you and, from there, ask yourself whether you've got the balance right.

• Step into first position. Ask yourself how *you* feel, what *you* want.

• Is it so very dreadful to have as much of a right to feelings and wants as the others involved?

- Examine why you think the others should be treated differently from yourself. Is there really a good enough reason?

- Step into third position and assess the situation again, this time giving yourself as much importance as anyone else.

RIDER PROFILES

Self-referenced

Ted is a strong and quite skilful rider, who enjoys his dressage. His old horse died recently, and he's been having some problems building a relationship with his new mare, Mandy. When he asks her to go in an outline Mandy rounds her neck all right, but she stiffens in the back. Ted thinks she's being difficult, but his trainer says he needs to ride her more gently and take time getting her trust. Ted thinks his trainer is being soft, and decides to look for someone else.

Josie is a teenager who's been quite successful in local jumping classes with her pony, Peppermint. Josie's parents are proud of her and suggest that, as she's beginning to outgrow Peppermint, it may be time to buy a horse instead – one who has the talent to take her on to bigger fences and better shows. But Josie says she doesn't want to stop riding Peppermint yet.

'I'll ride her until I'm too heavy for her, not just too tall', she says, 'and if that means stopping competing, that's fine by me. Pepper's my friend, and I'm never going to get rid of her.'

Other-referenced

Carrie rides regularly with her best friends from school. Although she is rather nervous, they persuade her to join them on a ten-mile sponsored ride. 'Go on, you'll enjoy it once you get there', they say. But, as the day draws closer, Carrie becomes more anxious. The night before, she can't sleep, and in the morning she doesn't want any breakfast. She doesn't say anything, because she doesn't want to let her friends down, and because people have promised money to her school for every mile she rides. So she goes, but feels really anxious. Her pony is tense and excited, and when someone else canters past on a long stretch he just takes off and hurtles after. Although she doesn't fall off, Carrie is terrified, and vows never to go on a long ride again. In fact, it even takes her several months to pluck up her courage to go on an ordinary hack.

Amanda is a quiet and serious person who works as a care assistant in a nursing home. In her spare time she rides, and when the local Riding Club was short of volunteer helpers for their dressage festival she said she'd help out. She spent the day collecting judges' sheets and helping with the scoring, and thoroughly enjoyed being useful and meeting so many people. When the organizer thanked her at the end of the day, Amanda said she'd willingly help another time. By the end of the season she had made a real contribution to the success of several events, and was asked if she'd be willing to be on the committee. Of course she agreed: 'It's good to be useful, and it's such fun', she said.

Orientation in Time

In-Time ——————————————————— Through-Time

One of the amazing things about the human mind is that it can travel in time. You can go forward into the future ('I know I'll be nervous and fail to do myself justice') or back into the past ('I can still feel that wonderful gallop'). You might be busy doing something here-and-now but fail to be truly present because you're off somewhere else in your head. As with all the other meta-programmes, there isn't one right way to be – only ways that are better and worse in the circumstances.

NLP has identified two very common patterns of experiencing time, and these have different implications for us as riders.

In-time

Some people are very in-the-moment. They are immersed in what's going on right now, whether in external events, or the internal experiences of their own minds and bodies. NLP calls this way of being **in-time**, for obvious reasons.

In-time pluses
People who are in-time are likely to pay really good attention to what they're involved in as it's happening. They will enjoy the good things, relish the successes as they occur, be in touch with what's going on. They will probably be very aware of the information they're getting through their senses, and how

they feel about it. Things will seem immediate, colourful and strong to them and they get really involved and committed.

In-time pitfalls
Because they are so 'in the moment', these people may find it hard to plan and, equally, they may find it difficult to learn from some past experiences because they've put these behind them. They can become stuck in a never-ending present, so projects that call for steady effort over time may fall by the wayside. They may tend to be late or to over-run, and can find it hard to prioritize.

Through-time

Another large grouping of people tend to take an overview of time, in which they experience the present moment in the context of what's gone before and what will come after. This is a **through-time** perspective.

Through-time pluses
These people find it easy to connect events in a cause-effect way, whether it's re-evaluating and learning from the past, or planning what to do now in relation to their future. This ability to connect may cushion them against immediate setbacks. They tend to be punctual and can keep to deadlines.

Through-time pitfalls
Because part of their attention is on the past and the future, they may not get quite so much out of the present. Equally, they may be so busy running past or future scenarios that they fail to take the actions needed in the present to make things happen – or, alternatively, to prevent them from happening! Other people may sometimes think in-time people rather remote or uninvolved.

In-time and Through-time Language

In-time	*Through-time*
Now	Overview
This moment/immediate	Longer perspective
Put the past behind me	Planning/scheduling
Look ahead to the future	Tomorrow/yesterday
Today	Future/past

Motivation

Tips for motivating yourself if you are predominantly an in-time person:
• Catch the moment – do it now.

• Notice what your senses are telling you.

• Get stuck in there.

Tips for motivating yourself if you are predominantly a through-time person:

• Set aside time to review and plan how things are progressing.

• Ask what you can learn from the past that will help you now.

• Consider how what you're doing now can build towards what you want in the future.

Stretching Yourself

Tips for stretching yourself if you are an in-time person. Guideline – spread the thread – link forwards and backwards:

• Ask yourself how the past can help you make wise choices, and how you can shape what you want in the future.

• Re-run events from the past to gather more information. Re-run things that went well to find out exactly how you got them right, and things that went badly so you know what to avoid today and in the future.

Tips for stretching yourself if you are a through-time person. Guideline – now is the hour:

• Now is the only time you can act. Zero in from your past learning and your future hopes. How can they help you this minute?

• Pay attention to here-and-now information: it's the basis for shaping your future.

• How you are now is the sum of all you have been. Take stock. Evaluate. Choose what to keep and what to change as you go forward.

RIDER PROFILES

In-time

When you're actually riding you need to zero in and be present, whatever your natural preference in the rest of your life. Many riders are naturally in-time, like Cathy, for whom hours pass like minutes when she's down at the yard. Her family have given up hope that she'll be back in time for lunch, even though she says she will and genuinely means to. Somehow, once she's there she gets absorbed. She gets chatting to friends while she does the stable work; she gets distracted while she's schooling. 'Feather-brain me', she says ruefully. She has great plans for schooling her young horse, Tigger, but her very enjoyment of his playful high spirits means that she often forgets what she intended to focus her schooling on. Then she gets really depressed because they haven't made the progress she hoped for. Getting him fit and trained for that Riding Club competition seems hopeless – though when the schedule came through she thought she had plenty of time. One day she's wildly optimistic about her riding, another she's in despair. 'I wish I wasn't so up and down', she thinks.

Sally is Cathy's friend at the yard, and she is also an in-time person. Sunny and bubbly, she just laughs when things go wrong. She has a natural talent as a rider, and really concentrates when she's riding. Like Cathy, she can't keep track of time when she's with the horses, but somehow she manages to use her in-time awareness to improve her riding. In fact, their teacher is urging her to start training as a dressage judge because she's really good at observing and reflecting on what she notices.

Through-time

Sandy and Steve keep their horses at the same place. They are hardworking managers in the same large organization, so they can only ride in the evenings and at weekends. Their diaries are highly planned, and they find it frustrating when something delays or interrupts their busy schedules. They approach their riding as they do their work: while they really enjoy it they know exactly what they want to achieve, and they plan and prepare carefully for the long distance rides and competitions that are their passion. Their ability to plan and pace themselves through time is a useful asset in long distance riding, and they are becoming quite successful. When friends ask them why on earth they rush about between work and the yard, with hardly a spare moment, and seem to drive themselves so hard, they say how restful they find it once they get to the horses. 'Time seems to expand once we're there, however stressed we've been', they say.

They are so enthusiastic about riding that they persuade their colleague, Henry, to come with them and have some lessons. But although Henry is a similarly through-time kind of person, he finds it impossible to get immersed in riding the way his friends do. He gets frustrated by how long it seems to be taking him to build up any skill and confidence, and doesn't like feeling so inept – even though he understands intellectually that any complex skill takes time to acquire. He's not used to being so 'in the moment' – particularly when the moment is uncomfortable, messy or intimidating. So he rapidly gives up.

Plotting Your Meta-programmes

In this chapter I've outlined how some of the key meta-programmes can affect our riding, and tried to illustrate through the rider profiles the NLP axiom that while there's nothing inherently 'good' or 'bad' about any pattern – even at the extreme ends – there can certainly be advantages and disadvantages. The art is to know your own natural preferences, to know how they help and hinder you, to use your strengths and to work at stretching yourself so that you can begin to use the less familiar kinds of patterning when they will help you. And I'd invite you to fill in the gaps in the chart below, so as to make a record you can use to help make the most of your natural assets and to construct a stretch programme for yourself.

- Put a X on each meta-programme axis to show your natural placing.

- Then fill in the strengths/limitations slots in terms of your riding.

- Next, work out what will help motivate you in terms of your programming.

- Finally, devise some stretch exercises for yourself. Get a friend, or your trainer, to help if necessary.

1. Preferred chunk size

Small ——————————————————————— **Large**

Strengths

_____

_____

Limitations

_____

_____

Motivation

_____

_____

Stretch Exercises

_____

_____

2. Direction of motivation

Towards ————————————————————— **Away From**

Strengths

_____

_____

Limitations

_____

_____

Motivation

_____

_____

Stretch Exercises

_____

_____

3. Options or procedures

Options ——————————————————— **Procedures**

Strengths

_____

_____

Limitations

_____

_____

Motivation

_____

_____

Stretch Exercises

_____

_____

4. Frame of reference

Internal ——————————————————— **External**

Strengths

_____

_____

Limitations

_____

_____

Motivation

_____

_____

Stretch Exercises

_____

_____

5. In-time ———————————————— **Through-time**

Strengths

_____

_____

Limitations

_____

_____

Motivation

_____

_____

Stretch Exercises

_____

_____

Building meta-programme profiles has other advantages, too. You can begin to understand just how it is that you seem to be on the same wavelength as some people – and, perhaps even more importantly, you can appreciate why others who function very differently think and behave as they do. You have a valuable tool for every sphere of your life, not just for riding.

In the next chapter I'm going to take the exploration of meta-programmes even further, and consider a very radical, and very exciting, possibility – that our horses have their own kind of meta-programmes, and that we can use this understanding of them to help manage the problems we may have with them and to create training which is tailored not only to our ambitions and their needs, but to their individual natures. Through NLP, we are able to take the intimate and everyday knowledge we have of our horses one stage further, acquiring for the first time a proven tool for understanding, training – and above all communicating – more effectively. And to my mind, that's really exciting.

Meta-programmes in Action – Working with Nicky M

When I was planning this book, I decided that it would be good to explore the effectiveness of a coaching approach not just with riders I already knew but with others whom I'd not previously worked with. So Nicky and her mare, Lucinda, were previously unknown to me. The case-studies at the end of the book explain more about how we came together and what kind of alliances we designed for our work. The agenda for the work was the rider's: my agenda was to use my NLP coaching skills to help each rider to clarify what they wanted and become more effective self-coaches when working on their own. Nicky and I decided that, because her goal was to achieve a change in her own feelings and behaviour, we would work on the telephone as well as with Nicky riding in the school. Because of this, we didn't have a single, specific, aim for Lucinda's schooling: our focus was on Nicky.

But of course, whenever you work with a rider you are also affecting the horse – in fact, as Charles de Kunffy said to me, 'You always work through the rider to the horse'. So we knew that whatever made a difference for Nicky would also make a difference for Lucinda, as indeed turned out to be the case.

Our second mounted session illustrates very clearly the part that meta-programmes play in riding, and it took Nicky and Lucinda well into their stretch zone – both figuratively and literally.

Nicky is highly motivated and conscientious in everything she does. She wants to do her best, and is impatient with any shortcomings or 'failures'. This, indeed, was at the core of the problem she wanted us to work on, as the case-study account in the final section of the book shows. For setting herself such high standards meant that Nicky found it hard to accept anything less than good riding in herself. She was more tolerant of Lucinda, who was sharp, and could be spooky, difficult and sometimes 'mareish'; but often she got frustrated and angry.

Lucinda is a five-year-old Warmblood, with expressive movement, and a lot of talent. She likes to go forward, and had been getting some good marks and favourable comments at Novice level in affiliated dressage competitions. This made it all the harder for Nicky on a 'bad day' and, because she is a very responsible person, she was inclined to blame herself. Because she is competitive by nature, she tended to judge herself and her horse in terms of success and failure. Success meant a smooth performance, being placed or winning. Failure meant 'messing up' a movement (i.e. doing it less well than Nicky knew they could), Lucinda being naughty or spooky, or Nicky losing her cool and ultimately pulling out of the test part-way through.

If we think of this profile in terms of the meta-programmes, it shows clearly how any pattern can have both strengths and limitations in practice. The very conscientiousness and high standards that make Nicky good in her job as a journalist – and promising as a rider working with a good young horse and an excellent dressage trainer – also meant that she didn't allow much leeway for learning, experimentation or mistakes. We could say that she tended towards the small chunk, procedural end of the spectrum, and that, while she had clear goals, the way she thought of them showed an 'away from' rather than a 'towards' motivation. She wanted to get it right, hated being wrong or in the wrong. Though highly motivated and a 'self-starter', she was externally referenced in that she cared a lot about how others would see her and how they would judge her.

So far as orientation in time goes, I'd say that Nicky usually took a through-time perspective, which enabled her to plan and to meet deadlines, essential for doing her job effectively. Of course this involved action and experience in the moment, and it's when things were difficult in the moment – especially in riding – that Nicky got thrown into an in-time sense of failure, anger and sometimes despair which she found unfamiliar, distressing and difficult to handle. It was the very opposite of the professionalism and competence which were so characteristic of her.

I'd gathered much of this from talking with Nicky and watching her ride the first time we met. When our second mounted session came around, I felt that it would be helpful to Nicky to emphasize a playful and experimental approach, and to set our goal as one of shared exploration and discovery rather than of achieving 'better' work or greater correctness. I had recently been watching my friend Marisian working our horses forward and stretching them through, and I thought this kind of work might help both Nicky and Lucinda to become looser, freer and more playful.

Judging dressage as frequently as I do, I'm often struck by the way that talented horses, who are soft and expressive horses at Novice level, can become tighter and more restricted as they compete at higher levels. It's likely that dressage as a discipline attracts people who are procedural rather than inventive, and it may also suit horses who are externally-referenced rather than internally-referenced. (See the next chapter for an exploration of how meta-programmes help us understand horses, too.) One quite unintentional by-product of the affinity between dressage and a procedural approach could be the loss of fluency and softness which often seems to accompany aiming for greater precision in the more advanced movements. Marisian's former trainer was quite unusual in asking her Grand Prix horses to do concentrated dressage only two days a week, while working them forward and low, or hacking them, the remaining days. I have also heard of another very successful trainer who regularly gallops his dressage horses across country to develop forwardness and balance, as well as fitness. But my guess is that many of us everyday dressage riders get unintentionally tramlined – by nature and circumstances – into offering our horses (and ourselves) a rather restricted diet of work. And this means that we end up by limiting versatility – both our own and our horses' – and perhaps even detracting from the very goal of apparently effortless athleticism that we are really aiming for.

When I asked Nicky at the beginning of our second mounted session what she wanted us to work on, she didn't have a specific problem or goal, so I asked her if she'd like to play around with working forward and down. I'd noticed from the photographs of the first session that Lucinda sometimes tended to overbend and fall behind the leg – a pattern which can easily be reinforced if the rider asks for an outline with more emphasis from the hand than from the leg. While Nicky's hands weren't restrictive, she had tended to ride Lucinda very quietly and not use much leg, because the mare was naturally forward-thinking and tended to be sharp and spooky. So this day it seemed like a good idea to experiment.

It's easy with hindsight to realize that asking Nicky to do this took her straight into her stretch zone, but because she's externally referenced and I was there to help her she didn't object, but just did her best to do what I asked. She said later that she found it quite difficult! First of all, Nicky felt insecure without rein contact – I'd asked her to give the rein away and really ride Lucinda 'through' until she made the contact for herself. Nicky was pleased to find that Lucinda didn't take advantage and tank off, spook or buck (all of which she half-expected), but then realized how much she'd been relying on the reins to steer. In particular, without reins to help her, Nicky couldn't get Lucinda to turn across the school to the right.

Being both polite and persevering, Nicky kept going, even though she was beginning to feel the familiar build-up of frustration and even anger, as she told me afterwards. Because her procedural, through-time programming made her willing to persevere, we were able to experiment until she found what helped Lucinda to understand what was wanted: a combination of more weight in Nicky's right stirrup and more turn through the waist and hips. And then Nicky's perseverance paid off and she got not only the specific result she wanted from Lucinda, but also the knowledge that she could use her leg,

above Giving the rein away – taking the risk in trot.

left Giving the rein away in a subsequent session – more risky in canter, but Lucinda remains attentive and balanced.

weight and seat effectively. Allowing herself to do what she initially found difficult, which was to go beyond what she naturally found comfortable and to experiment, brought Nicky an increased confidence in herself and enhanced her ability to communicate effectively with her horse.

Working to stretch your natural and familiar meta-programme behaviour may feel strange or even cause temporary insecurity, as it did for Nicky. But it's worth experimenting because it can expand and enrich the choices you have available. One of the fundamental discoveries in the early days of NLP was that the person with the greatest flexibility of thought and behaviour in any situation has the greatest potential influence. By taking the risk of going beyond the familiar, you give yourself the opportunity not only of growth, but also of obtaining greater leverage. And if you make sure that you stretch yourself bit by bit, with whatever support you need and in ways you find do-able without undue stress, then your experiments in stretching should be as rewarding as Nicky's.

6

Motivating Your Horse

A S I SHOWED IN THE previous chapter, knowing about meta-programmes gives us invaluable information about how we characteristically process information internally and how we react to external events. If NLP as a whole is 'the brain-user's guide', meta-programmes are one of its key sections. It's important that we gather, and use, information about our meta-programmes in a spirit of non-judgemental curiosity. This attitude is at the core of coaching, and self-coaching, because it helps us to keep focused on effects rather than either blaming ourselves or seeking to pat ourselves on the back. A success/failure way of framing things has its own pitfalls – even if we feel we're getting things right – as I'll explain in the next chapter.

So, to recap: whatever your characteristic meta-programme tendencies, they will be an asset to you in certain circumstances, and may limit you in others. And the same is true for your horse.

Up till now, no one has thought of suggesting that animals have meta-programmes, yet every horse-owner could give a character profile of their horse and his normal ways of behaving. (The same is true, I believe, of dog-owners.) So that's why this chapter is perhaps more hypothetical than others in the book. It's an attempt to break new ground by exploring how NLP can help us to understand non-human subjects.

I'd like to ask you to follow me in imagining, for the moment, that horses do have their own patterns of reacting to experience and processing it, and that some of these are not dissimilar from ours in the way they sort for certain kinds of information. I'm suggesting that we can learn a lot about our horses by assuming that their natural ways of making sense of the world, like ours, seek out certain kinds of information and deal with it in a range of ways that fall somewhere between opposite extremes. I think they are governed by their own version of meta-programmes.

As NLP reminds us, it can be very helpful at times to act as though something were the case, rather than necessarily believing it to be a 'fact'. Where you find a particular 'as-if' helpful to you, it's worth learning from it: where it doesn't seem helpful, ask yourself why and perhaps find yourself adding something to the sum of human understanding. That's how new discoveries take place. And because I'm putting forward for the first time the idea that horses have their own meta-programmes, I'd be glad of your comments and your examples. That way, you make the idea of greater validity and greater value, as it acquires more 'evidence' gets shared with a wider audience.

When you or I describe our horses, we often talk of them as characters. 'He's touchy.' 'She's sharp.' 'He gets confused by new things.' 'She's really laid-back whatever's going on.' So what is a character? Whether it's human or animal, it's essentially a patterning of behaviour that is recognizable and habitual to the person or animal being described. Apart from physical appearance, it's an important part of what differentiates one from another. Think how many chestnut (or bay) horses there are – and yet how each one is distinctive once you know them. At one time our two chestnuts were in a yard composed entirely of chestnut horses. Sometimes when we saw them at a distance out in the field we had to count white socks, or look for distinctive profiles, to tell which was which. Yet none of the owners would have had any difficulty telling them apart through their behaviour in the stable or their reactions in the school.

While, in the previous chapter, I've outlined some key meta-programmes separately for the sake of clarity, of course in reality what makes any one of us distinctive is the particular combinations in which we cluster them – in other words, our individual profile. Let's start this chapter, then, with a brief profile of the horse you know best. It could be one you own, or ride regularly. It could be one you knew well in the past.

> Describe your chosen horse in a few sentences, just as you might quickly do to someone who said: 'What's your horse like?' Put down what comes quickly and easily into your mind. Don't, at this point, feel that you should remember or match this profile with the meta-programmes as such. You're looking for things like characteristic reactions, behaviours, skills and difficulties, likes and dislikes.

Profiling Your Horse's Meta-programmes

Now let's see how useful the meta-programme profiling is in helping you understand the basis for your horse's characteristic patterns, and in making links between them and the way he or she responds to you and your teaching. I'm going to draw upon the same key meta-programmes as I did in the previous chapter, with the exception of the in-time/through time orientation. I doubt whether anyone knows how horses experience time – though I'd welcome any ideas or evidence you may have. And, of course, there's an important difference between building up human and equine meta-programme profiles. We can ask other people to tell us about their thoughts and feelings, in the same way as the early developers of NLP used questions as part of the modelling process that helped them to formulate the observations and information that became NLP. But, in the case of animals, we have to rely on external observation of their behaviour and reactions – and that, in turn, means that we are liable to notice what we expect to notice. It may even mean that we interpret what we observe in the light of our own meta-programme preferences! Researchers know that there's no such thing as 'pure' or truly 'objective' research. But it's the best we can do, and it's certainly good enough – because, if we are wrong, events will provide us with further information, and we can correct or refine our findings.

For each meta-programme, I'm going to offer some ideas about the kind of tell-tale behaviour that indicates each end of the spectrum. Then I'm going to illustrate this from observations of a horse I know. And finally, I'm going to suggest some ways in which you might use this knowledge to help you in training your particular horse.

In the previous chapter, I offered you some ideas for stretching yourself towards your least-favourite way of processing. That's because I know you have the capacity to learn, change and grow if you want to. However, in exploring the training implications of the different meta-programmes here, I'm going to stick with ways of harnessing your horse's natural preferences. I think it likely that animals could be helped to stretch, if they had the motivation and trusted their rider/trainer sufficiently. But I also think that there is plenty for us to do before we have exhausted the possibilities for harnessing how they already work. And this, too, is in keeping with the discoveries of NLP and the principles of coaching.

One of the central observations that arose from modelling really effective communicators was that they all 'paced' the people they were working with before seeking to influence or 'lead' them in any way. **Pacing** is a central and subtle concept, which involves conveying the message that we are truly 'with' the other being with whom we are communicating. We can pace by literally going at the same speed in our movement, even down to breathing at the same rate as them. We can pace by using the same language. We can pace by going along with how they are and what they are doing. We can pace their meta-programme preferences, once we have recognized what they are. However, pacing is more than just 'going along with'. It doesn't mean that you never confront, disagree or discipline. It means that you seek to work from within the other being's framework. And so far as training your horse is concerned, if you pace not only his physical energy and state of well-being but also his meta-programme preferences, the acceptance and understanding this conveys to him will put him in the best state for rapport and for learning with you. Pacing is the essential foundation for leading – with meta-programmes as with everything else.

Preferred Chunk Size

Small ————————————————————— **Large**

Likely characteristics of a small chunk horse
May get anxious when a lot is going on – can become overwhelmed. May seem more secure when he can grasp or do things step by step.

Likely characteristics of a large chunk horse
Gets the idea quickly. Anticipates routines from slight indicators (whether in the stable or in the school). May over-anticipate and not 'listen'. May 'guess'.

HORSE PROFILES

Small Chunk

Georgie Boy is one of the horses I've been working with for the case-studies in this book, and there's more about how his rider, Sean, and I worked with him in the written-up session that follows this chapter and at the end of the book. Georgie seems to prefer small-chunk information. Sean told me that Georgie 'likes to think things through – in fact he can think too much'. New manoeuvres have to be explained to him bit by bit or he gets anxious and panics. When we started to work together, Georgie was having trouble learning walk pirouettes because he didn't really understand exactly what he had to do. So he tended to 'stick' and just stop.

Georgie tended to 'stick' and stop in the pirouette because he didn't understand.

Our older horse, Lolly, enjoys jumping – provided you build up from a pole on the ground via a series of jumps gradually increasing in height. If you ask him to jump a pole even as low as eighteen inches without this preparation he will stop.

Large Chunk

My younger horse Vals likes larger chunks, and this preference produces problems of its own. Once he knows how to do something, he is calm and laid-back. But when he's being taught something he tends to have a bash at what he thinks is wanted – sometimes when it isn't! He picks up from his rider that something is going to happen, and then just guesses. He finds it difficult to wait and listen for specific instructions. When he was learning simple changes he used to get so anxious that he would stop and sometimes even go backwards after a canter-walk transition because he couldn't bear not knowing what came next.

Training theme

Chunk size issues all have to do with the relationship between parts and the whole.

Tips for working with small chunk horses

• Build up step by step.

• Teach each step in isolation. Only go on to the next one when your horse has really understood the previous one.

Tips for working with large chunk horses

- Whenever you can, 'arrange' for him to experience a new manoeuvre as a whole – and successfully – so that he gets the whole experience, and gets it right. Many trainers teach flying changes by riding across the diagonal so that the correct lead becomes the wrong lead and the horse changes naturally. This can backfire if he only changes in front, or behind, and doesn't get the whole picture. But often getting what's wanted, even if it's rough-and-ready, allows a large-chunker to get a general idea, which you can then polish.

- Disguise the build-up of learning. Separate the steps, both in time and in physical location, so that he is free to concentrate calmly and doesn't try to guess what comes next.

Direction of Motivation

Towards ———————————————————— **Away From**

Likely characteristics of a 'towards' horse
Will 'have a go'. Tends to be bold in approach, forward-going and enthusiastic. May be overbold or careless. May enjoy new experiences or situations and be curious about them rather than alarmed. Will like praise, and may not respond well to being corrected.

Likely characteristics of an 'away from' horse
When in doubt, will flee. May be easily distracted or intimidated by new or unknown things and experiences. Becomes anxious when he 'gets things wrong'. Responds to disapproval and is fearful of punishment. May be easily cowed, by bossy humans or other horses. May need reassurance. Careful.

HORSE PROFILES

Towards

When I was a student on vacation, I used to borrow a pony from the farm just up the lane from my parents' house in Somerset. Rosewood was about 13.2hh and game for anything. She enjoyed hacking, and was interested in anything and everything when we were out together. Her head was never still as she looked this way and that. She would sniff gates and hedgerows like a dog, and enjoyed keeping time as I sang her rousing choruses from opera or soldiers' marching songs

---

from the First World War. She had low withers and when I got fed up shifting her saddle every time it moved onto her shoulder she was quite happy for me to hack her bareback. She was an enthusiastic, 'towards' person.

Away From

Our older horse, Lolly, is very cautious. He likes to take a good look at anything new – even a trotting pole on the ground, although he's been over them many times before. He actually likes jumping – but he has to check his fences out first! When we first had him, my daughter and husband took him to a Riding Club cross-country practice. Lolly did jump all the obstacles, including a small stream, but only after considering each one from a standstill first. Only after this inspection was he prepared to go back and take a run at any fence. When something unexpected happens, like a bird flying up beside the school, Lolly's first instinct is to leap sideways away from the 'danger', and then charge off in a fast canter. He's quite prepared to be reassured and brought back to a calmer pace – once he's got away from the enemy.

Training theme

Ask yourself if your horse is drawn towards carrots or driven by sticks.

Tips for working with a 'towards' motivation

- Pace your horse's enjoyment of new things, and give him variety so that he doesn't get bored.

- Give him toys to play with in his box.

- Change activity and direction (literally) frequently, so that you keep his attention on you and on what he's doing.

- Vary his work so that he isn't asked to spend all his time on your major discipline.

- Make your training interesting but also challenging, so that he learns to listen to you rather than making up his own mind and ignoring you.

- Develop ways of letting him know when you do want him to make up his own mind. For example, when you want him to wait for you to tell him to take off, regulate his natural stride as you start your approach to the fence, keep him gathered together and give him a clear take-off signal with your legs (backed up, perhaps, by your voice). When you want him to use his own initiative, you might use less contact and just follow his natural stride.

Tips for working with 'away from' motivation

• Give plenty of praise.

• Respect his feelings of alarm but don't let yourself get panicked by him.

• Don't punish his panic – he isn't setting out to be naughty. He's just a flight animal whose flight response is close to the surface.

• Make it clear to him when he gets things right and when he gets them wrong – but don't put much emotion into it as that confuses and alarms him. A pat for 'Yes' and a quiet 'No' for no, followed by a clearer 'explanation' of how he is to achieve what you want, will usually be enough.

• Don't overface him – his confidence will take a long time to recover. Work mostly within his safety zone and make it as safe and encouraging as you can for him to do things which stretch him.

Method of Approach

Options ———————————————— Procedures

Likely characteristics of an 'options' horse
Tolerates new experiences, new situations, new tasks well. Is curious about new things. Not bothered by changes of routine. May get bored easily and, when bored, may get stroppy or switch off. May be rather 'gung-ho'.

Likely characteristics of a 'procedures' horse
Dislikes change in routines. Learns routines easily and repeats them, sometimes without being asked. Has a good memory for something once learnt. May be anxious about change. Accurate and precise.

HORSE PROFILES

Mainly Options
Our first horse, Tristan, was a mixture of pure Thoroughbred and Warmblood. In temperament, he was more like his Thoroughbred sire. He hotted up quickly, and

---

when he did, he tended to lose focus and cease to pay attention to his rider. Trained in dressage before we had him, he was skilled in the movements but got more tense the more was asked of him. He was great as a first horse because he enjoyed variety. Jumping turned out to be an unexpected skill and he adored it. He was happy (and tireless) when we took him on long distance rides, and he enjoyed hacking in company. As we got better at dressage, Tristan tended to get wound-up and excited. Temperamentally he was an options person – but options excited him. Routines calmed him. He loved being in the horse walker, and nowadays enjoys a very laid-back, uneventful life in retirement, his days varied only by being turned out and brought in, fed, rugged and watered. He is a good illustration of both the strengths and limitations of his meta-programming.

Procedures

One of the case-studies in my previous book (*Schooling Problems Solved with NLP*) was of Karen and her horse, Billy. Billy's pattern of life was quite ordered, and this suited both him and Karen (who also prefers procedures). Billy got used to patterns of being turned out and brought in, and he readily learnt to stale when Karen whistled. This meant that she could ask him to go in the field before bringing him in, which saved expense on bedding. Billy enjoyed a regular hack, and being turned out in the field with his friends.

Training theme

Whether things are organized with a view to choice or to repeated procedures.

Tips for harnessing an options preference

• Provide variety – of activity, of surroundings, of tasks.

• Use frequent change to match your horse's enjoyment of different options.

• Avoid constant repetition, as this will bore him and lose his attention. Doing something again and again is likely to make for a worse, not a better, performance.

Tips for harnessing a procedural preference

• Teach and habituate your horse into the patterns you want. Reinforce his learning through repetition and praise. Let him enjoy the feeling of being 'good'.

- Remember that he will learn any pattern easily – ones you don't want just as easily as ones you do!

- Think about what he may be learning 'by accident' A procedural horse will learn a pattern much faster than an options-oriented one, so be careful not to reinforce undesirable patterns accidentally, in the yard or in the school.

Source of Reference

Internal ——————————————————————— **External**

Likely characteristics of an internally (self-) referenced horse
Can be bold, courageous and fun. May not always 'listen' to his rider. Not easily influenced by praise or correction. Can be wilful or stubborn. Wants to do what he wants to do, when he wants to do it. May tend to argue with his rider. Can be cheeky or pushy. May be dominant in the field among his herd of friends. Has clear likes and dislikes.

Likely characteristics of an externally (other-) referenced horse
Likes to please. Hates being told off. May be less dominant, or even bullied, in the herd, and tends to regard his rider as though he or she were a superior horse. Can be passive, and will 'switch off' rather than rebelling. Needs a lead from his rider. Likes to know what's wanted so he can get things right.

HORSE PROFILES

Self-referenced

Nikki's horse, Merlin, was gelded late and retains some of his stallion attitude. He is territorial about the field where he used to be turned out when he was a colt (his 'stallion paddock') and quite rough in play when he's turned out in a different field with other horses. He's inclined to show off and pull at their headcollars or rugs. He is forward-going and powerful, and seems happier when he's being ridden by a dominant rider rather than a hesitant one. Sometimes he just isn't in the mood for paying attention, however skilled the rider, and then he can be stroppy and sullen.

Other-referenced

Our younger horse, Vals, is unusually other-referenced. In over five years since we bought him, he has only twice bucked under saddle – and both times he was

---

alarmed by something unexpected. Yet, when he's turned out in the field, his first response is to charge off at a gallop, bucking hugely. He will also buck on the lunge – now that he knows we aren't going to tell him off for it. He behaves like a foal around other horses, wanting to play and pestering them to join in. When they get fed up with this he tends to get bitten or kicked, like the runt of the herd. He hates being told off, and will switch off and cease to go forward rather than argue. If he doesn't know what's wanted, he tends to panic and guess.

Training theme

Relate to whose influence the horse looks to for guidance, decisions, or when in doubt.

Tips for working with internally (self-) referenced horses

• Accept your possible role as a superior horse – but don't overdo it.

• Try to avoid showdowns – it's not good for either of you and could be dangerous.

• Where you can, let him use his initiative, and praise it.

• Make doing what you want seem like doing what he wants. Look for win-win scenarios. Use schooling patterns to make it easy for him to do what you want – then praise him.

Tips for working with externally (other-) referenced horses

• Make it easy for him to 'get it right' by communicating clearly and showing him what's wanted. Praise him lavishly.

• Give him some time off during which he doesn't have to be especially good for you. If he's a dressage specialist, do some jumping and hacking. Let him have time off in the field, so that he can relax and do his own thing. If he's normally asked to be an accurate showjumper, play with a bit of distance work or cross-country. Make it all right to have fun and experiment together. You'll have to take the lead to show him that it's acceptable.

Meta-programme Clustering

Once we start to apply the idea of meta-programmes to horses, it will become apparent that horses, like people, tend to favour certain clusterings. It's likely that a 'towards' horse will also be an 'options' horse, and that an 'away from' horse may also be externally referenced. There are always exceptions, and getting to understand how your horse functions in these terms gives you information that can help you both get more enjoyment from your work and play together.

> Now go back to your original sketch of your horse's personality. What seem to be his meta-programme preferences – and how do these help explain his strengths and limitations? In the light of this way of understanding him, are there changes you need to make, or want to make, to improve the way you train him so as to make it easier for you both?

Assessing the Horse/Rider Match

There's one more question to ask yourself at this stage. Now that you've thought about your own meta-programme preferences and those of your horse – are you a good match? Having similar preferences may explain why you get on so well – and it may also explain some of your strengths and limitations as a pair. If you are different in some respects, you may now have information that helps you resolve some of your difficulties. In an extreme case, it's possible that you may understand why you are unhappy with your partnership.

> Take a few moments to explore the 'fit' between you and your horse in meta-programme terms, and to think about its implications for now and for the future.

As with humans, all kinds of partnerships can work, not just those between individuals who think and respond alike. You and your horse may complement and enjoy each other even if you are different. But if you are different and don't enjoy each other, you may now have some information that makes it easier for you to take that difficult decision to let him go – and that helps you to make a more appropriate choice next time.

Meta-Programmes in Action II – Working with Georgie Boy

At the beginning of our first session with Georgie, Sean said he'd welcome my help with walk pirouettes since Georgie was finding it difficult to get the idea of what was involved. Georgie was just beginning to compete at Medium level, where walk pirouettes are first required. A good pirouette is one where the horse keeps an even, marching walk rhythm throughout, describing a very small circle with his hind legs while drawing a larger circle around them with his forehand. The smaller the pirouette circle, the better – provided the walk is maintained. Common faults are losing the rhythm, missing a step behind (sticking), and stepping wide behind (i.e. swinging around with the horse's weight over his centre rather than his quarters).

When Georgie was warmed up, Sean showed me some pirouettes. Georgie tended to lose the walk and to stick behind – and sometimes he also stuck in front and stopped altogether! As the photograph shows, Georgie's expression seems puzzled. He's not rebelling – he simply doesn't understand.

Knowing that Georgie likes to think things through bit by bit, Sean had tried doing quarter- and half-pirouettes to help him build the idea gradually.

Puzzled pirouette.

He had also ridden into a corner and asked Georgie for a quarter-pirouette facing the fence (i.e. turning 45 degrees from his approach), so that this would encourage Georgie to move his forehand around his hindquarters naturally. Mostly, these attempts went well – but when Sean asked for a full pirouette Georgie either stuck or spun round in a small circle.

I noticed that, because Sean didn't want Georgie to stop, he tended to ask for the pirouette by leaning back and collecting the walk on his weight and his hand. The effect of this was to spin Georgie round – and still he didn't always make the full turn. In order to match Georgie's preference for small chunk learning, I suggested that Sean concentrate on one of the building blocks of the pirouette rather than the pirouette itself – in other words, helping Georgie to collect himself and 'sit' while still moving forward. (This will also be an essential foundation for canter pirouettes later in Georgie's career.) Although Georgie is a large and heavy horse, he is quite light on his feet, and responded well when Sean drew himself up taller and half-halted through flattening his shoulder-blades. Practising this in walk, trot and canter improved Georgie's engagement and helped him to lighten in front.

The aim of our work together – as with all the case-study riders – was to raise ideas which Sean could use when working on his own, and to hammer out together some guidelines for self-coaching. So I was very pleased to hear, when I next saw Sean, that the pirouettes had been going better. Sean said he found that drawing himself up taller and lightening his seat, instead of using a heavier seat to pin the quarters down, really seemed to help Georgie to keep the walk active, and Sean had then been able to bring the forehand around in a small circle without losing rhythm or stopping.

With Georgie, going back to smaller chunks really seemed to help. In the same session, we took a similar approach to flying changes, which were also a new task. Like many horses, Georgie had got the idea of changing in front but hadn't managed a complete or clean change. Because he's athletic and supple, he could quite easily continue cantering disunited for two enthusiastic circles afterwards, as the photo shows! Even asking for the change when approaching a corner across the diagonal, which Sean had tried, had not helped Georgie achieve a clean change – although this is often a successful strategy with a large-chunk learner.

Chunking down, I asked Sean what aids he used for an ordinary canter transition: I wondered whether Georgie's confusion started there. Sean told me that he used both his inside leg on the girth and his outside leg behind the girth when asking Georgie to canter. I remembered watching Arthur Kottas helping riders to teach flying changes on many occasions. Arthur always tells his pupils that they should train the horse to canter just by moving the outside leg back.

Disunited suppleness.

Because this is a single signal the horse will find it clearer than receiving signals from both legs, and thus easier to learn multiple changes later on in training. In NLP terms, learning how to respond to a single signal is a small chunk, which can then help to initiate a sequence of behaviours that together build up into a bigger chunk – in this case, the flying change. The series of changes required at the higher levels may seem to the rider to be a bigger chunk still, because they may think of the series of four-, three-, or two-time changes as a single manoeuvre. In fact, it may be more useful to think of each change as a separate, small chunk. As the next chapter shows, how you frame something in your mind sets up what happens, and framing something as a series – for example, a series of five x four-time changes – may well seem more daunting and difficult than thinking of each change as a separate event, interspersed with some 'ordinary' canter strides. And if, through taking the latter approach, the rider is calmer, so too will be the horse.

During the remainder of this working session, Sean practised asking for canter transitions with the outside leg aid only. When I saw them for our next session, Sean said that Georgie had been much lighter and calmer in his strike-offs than he had been when both legs were used.

Breaking new learning down into small chunks is often useful – and in Georgie's case it matches his small-chunk processing, and makes learning easier for him. It also means he has every chance of getting each step in the process 'right' – and thus his responses are reinforced through praise.

7

The Importance of Framing

Have you ever had the experience of suddenly changing your opinion of something, or feeling quite differently about it, just because of something someone said, or because you got a new piece of information? We are bombarded by information all the time, and in order to make meaning out of it all we rely on linking and clustering things together. We use categories. We make assumptions. We have our own mental filing systems, which are distinctive to us and not exactly the same as anyone else's, even if there are strong similarities. When you or I get a new piece of information that doesn't quite 'fit' with something we've filed in our own way, it may surprise or confuse or even anger us – but above all it makes us realize that there's more than one way of seeing things.

NLP calls these processes of mental categorizing and recategorizing **framing** and **reframing**. The image that a picture contains is given definition and meaning by its frame: change the frame, and you change the 'meaning' of the picture, even though you don't change the image. Different frames draw attention to different aspects of the image. To examine this point, let's go back to an example from an earlier chapter.

Susie the all-rounder described herself as being 'jack-of-all-trades and master of none' – a common enough phrase, and one that is rather downputting. It implies that you can be one or the other, but not both, and that it's somehow better to be a master. What if she had said, instead, that she was 'jack-of-all-trades, *not* master of one'? The words seem to mean the same, but the effect is to imply that she had a choice, and that, for her, it's better to enjoy a range of activities and skills.

This is an example of a verbal frame and reframe – and verbal reframes are quick to shift meanings, as many jokes, puns and advertisements illustrate. However, framing isn't just visual, like the picture, or verbal like the catch-phrase. It can also happen with our other senses. I'm sure that there have been times when you left the yard only to become aware as you changed to a non-horsy environment how strongly your clothes smelt. While you were at the yard your clothes smelt exactly the same – you just didn't notice. Changing environment caused a reframe – in this case, an olfactory one – as you noticed the smell. The change of context caused you to select a different meaning from the same available information: at the yard, the smell was acceptable because it was in context, whereas when you went shopping, or even when you got home, it was not. You are also quite likely, if you ride regularly, to have got used to various muscular aches, probably to the extent that you hardly notice them. Yet if you had a similar ache or pain without having been riding, you might be searching for a deep heat cream or even making an appointment with the doctor. Riding regularly means that you've learnt to change – that is, reframe – what you understand by 'normal' feelings in your muscles. This is a kinesthetic reframe, that is, it relates to physical sensation.

In this chapter I am going to look at the importance of framing in how you think of your riding, and explore how you can use reframing as a tool for self-coaching. And I want to add in another concept which NLP identified – that of **complex equivalents**. This label sounds rather abstract, but what it describes is both everyday and very powerful. A complex equivalent is all the specific meanings that someone attaches to an abstract term. 'Love', 'kindness', 'loyalty' all share complex equivalents. So too are concepts like 'throughness', 'forwardness' or 'being on the bit'. The problem is that, while we can all use the apparently simple word and think we're talking about the same thing, in fact we are each likely to have subtly different shades of meaning, or complex equivalents, for it. That's where trouble can start. And when you put framing and complex equivalents together, you've got a very powerful combination, which can work to enable you or to hinder you in numerous ways, both in your communication with others and in your own mind.

Let's take an example. If you think of your own riding and that of your trainer, do you ever think something like 'Well, I'm not bad *for an amateur*', or

'Throughness' – a complex equivalent that sums up many things: activity, balance, power from behind connecting through the back to the neck, head and mouth... Marisian and Prudie.

'*She's a professional*, so she's bound to ride better/win more competitions/ be more effective as a trainer/get run away with less often than me'? You're working with complex equivalents for 'amateur' and 'professional' here, and it may well be that these are framing your riding in a way that limits your effectiveness. If you assume that professionals are better than amateurs, it probably follows that you think there are some things you'll never be able to achieve as well – or perhaps even at all. It may mean that you defer to your trainer's judgement about your horse, even though you see him every day and have known him for years and she's only seen him once a week since you started lessons with her last January. And although it is appropriate to listen to what she says, if you automatically assume that she's right and you're wrong, you're allowing your own personal experience and your opinion to become of secondary importance for a reason which is partly hidden and which may not actually be valid. Usually, when a complex equivalent is involved it means we regard something as a fact, and we may not examine evidence relating to it or contradicting it – and that's when we can get into trouble.

The Curiosity Frame

Let's have a look at some broad ways of framing which are relevant to us as riders. Coaching and NLP share an important way of framing things. They frame them with an attitude of curiosity. And that's because they are essentially outcome-oriented in their approach. They're interested in exploring what happens; *when*, *where* and *how* it happens. If you approach things in this way, with this perspective, you regard a great many things as information. You are less likely to make black-and-white judgements. You are less likely to get into emotional reactions, whether negative or positive. A curiosity frame is a great one for learning and for teaching – whether it's yourself, someone else or the horse you're working with. Curiosity helps you to notice more, and wonder more about what you've noticed. It puts you into a detective mode. It makes you a researcher. It opens up new information, and new connections between information, as I suggested earlier in the book.

The Success/Failure Frame

The curiosity frame sets you up for very different experiences from those engendered by the commonly experienced success/failure frame. Curiosity is intensely focused but emotionally neutral. The success/failure frame, on the other hand, burdens you with judgements and with feeling good or bad about how you're doing. It opens up emotional reactions – and even 'good' feelings can block your search for new information. And unfortunately teaching – even good teaching – can set you up for success/failure, because it normally pays attention to learning how to do something well or correctly, and tells you when you're doing it badly, incorrectly, or not enough. There's another issue, too. The success/failure frame usually relies on what's true and trusted: expertise is something you recognize in others and aspire to for yourself. But, even when you've achieved what you want, a success/failure frame can stop you continuing your search for solutions and improvements.

There's an interesting contrast here with the curiosity frame, which all the time opens up further searching and promotes the discovery of further information. And why settle for one way of doing things, even if it works, when curiosity might tell you how and why it works, and help you experiment to find even more ways that work?

If you compete, of course, you're more or less set up for a success/failure frame. *Or are you?* It depends on how you frame competition itself. If winning is your badge of success, then you're quite likely to have bought into the corresponding belief that *not* winning means a degree of failure. Perhaps you'll allow yourself to accept that being placed will be enough – but even this may mean that, when you aren't, you pay less attention to your experience of how your horse went, and maybe overlook what he did well. This is often particularly true of 'recreational' competitors, because they may attach more weight to the opinions of judges than professionals do. When you're a professional, you probably ride more horses and compete more often, so you may be more likely to develop a healthy scepticism about judges and more trust in your own experience.

In *Schooling Problems Solved with NLP* I quoted Charles de Kunffy's view that we should think of competition as 'schooling away from home', and see it as another opportunity of benefiting the horse. This is a change in framing, which can have profound effects.

WHEN NICKY WENT TO HER first competition after we had begun working together, Lucinda spooked badly at the beginning of the dressage test. In the past, this would probably have resulted in Nicky retiring – a pattern which she had told me she wanted to change through working together for our case-study. Whereas on previous occasions Nicky had tended to chunk up and feel the whole test was ruined if anything went wrong, now she was able in a few crucial seconds to remind herself that one movement wasn't the whole test. She told herself that she and Lucinda both had plenty of ability, and that it was part of their learning together to overcome glitches like spooking. In talking together, I'd pointed out that horses don't carry forward feelings of disappointment or irritation with themselves: that's something riders do. Even their anxiety can usually be reduced pretty quickly if the rider is calm and focused. This meant that, if Nicky could recover her own concentration, she'd probably be able to get Lucinda's back, too. So when it came to this test, even though Nicky felt angry and disappointed, she put these feelings aside and focused on what they had to do next. The result was that Lucinda took the lead from her rider, regained her own concentration and did the rest of the test well. When Nicky's colleagues at work asked her next day how she'd done, they were amazed at her triumphant 'We came third!' For Nicky, being placed was still important – but she'd reframed 'success' to include overcoming difficulties, and she was genuinely delighted that she'd been able to think and behave differently.

The change that Nicky had made in her thinking and behaviour involved her changing the complex equivalent she had for 'success'. She still wanted to win – but she was able to be pleased with a place because she now realized that getting placed involved a different kind of success – that of regaining her own focus and that of her horse. Success now has a broader range of meanings for her.

And this is the point I want to make: a success/failure frame isn't 'bad' – it just has certain limitations. If you and your horse are doing well, be justly proud of yourselves – but don't pin everything on external benchmarks. Cultivate your own ability to judge your progress, and the degree to which it matches up with your aspirations. This gives you a realistic, self-referenced cushion when things go badly for you, or when someone misjudges or under-values you.

Sometimes you may be even more exacting in assessing yourself than an outsider would be, and that's fine so long as it's true to your honest experience. But when you felt something was good, and you've tested that out by examining the available evidence honestly, don't let external judgement override what you 'know' inside. A judge or trainer may tell you that your horse could do better – but don't let that spoil your pleasure in knowing that he's done his best to date, or that he's improved on how he went last week.

Moving from a Success/Failure Frame into a Curiosity Frame

Indicators of a Success/Failure Frame

- Words and phrases like:

do well	do badly	come top	achieve
made it	let down	disaster	triumph
good	bad	poor	fair

- Feeling elated when you get a high mark, and awful when you don't.

- Judging your worth and that of your horse according to placings, progress and marks.

- Envying others who have 'better' horses.

- Automatically accepting the views of people who are 'better' or who are in positions of authority.

- Waiting for others to tell you how well you're doing.

Tips for Getting into a Curiosity Frame

Ask yourself questions like:

What happens if...?

What's going on...?

What's this about...?

How am I causing/contributing to/preventing this?

How come he's responding like this?

When he does that, what does he think I'm asking for?

What next?

What else...?

What tells me that?

The 'As-if' Frame

NLP and coaching are both systemic in their approach: that is, they are based on the belief that human beings are made up of many interconnecting systems. A change in one system will inevitably have repercussions in others, whether it's anxiety that causes physical tension, joyfulness that leads to relaxation, a minor illness that leads to slow reactions, or framing that leads to certain expectations – and thus certain behaviours – rather than others.

Framing things 'as-if...' (for example, as-if something was true, as-if you could do it, as-if it were going to happen) can be a powerful way of helping you to achieve what you want. This is because it's a way of activating knowledge that you may not have known you had – or, if you did know, you may have felt you lacked the ability to use. Because of the interconnections between thought, feelings and behaviour, what we think or believe has a huge influence on what we do and how we do it, and in riding, the 'as-if' frame can be particularly helpful in unlocking skills – whether mental or physical – that may have been closed off by our beliefs.

Think of yourself as a pupil having a lesson. Notice what you feel emotionally, and how you are physically. Now think of yourself as a trainer, helping someone less knowledgeable or less experienced – even if you have never done this. What changes do you notice, in emotion, in thought, and in your body itself? What changes do you notice in your horse?

You have in your mind a great deal of information about what's involved in both of these roles – information gathered from personal experience as well as from many other sources. Just thinking of the label puts you in touch with what's involved, not only at a level of action but in terms of how it feels. You may never have actually taught someone else riding, but you will almost certainly have explained something at some time to someone else, even if it's just giving directions of a very simple kind. And because that information is stored in your brain, when you tap into it you gain access to what's involved at many levels. That's because the brain doesn't distinguish between what's factually 'real' and what isn't: anything that engages the brain is internally real to it, even if you then label it 'imagination' or 'something that happened to someone else'. So when you think 'as-if' you were a trainer, it activates different information, attitudes, feelings and behaviour from what's activated when you think 'as-if' you were a pupil.

Think of a skill that you've seen in action, perhaps someone riding a great showjumping or cross-country round, or a movement at dressage you've never attempted. Spend a few moments or even minutes imagining it as vividly as you can. Notice whether you're seeing it in your mind's eye, feeling it in your body as though you were doing it yourself, perhaps hearing the accompanying sounds... While each of us tends to rely more on one or two of our senses in these internal scenarios (NLP calls them **representations**), we can all potentially have access to the full range of our senses when we 'imagine'. So use what comes naturally to you.

Now change your representation slightly: put yourself in the picture, feel the feelings in your body, see out of your eyes as you ready, steady and go for that fence, glide across the arena in that fluent half-pass... And enrich the scenario by adding material from your other senses. Have sound and physical sensation and vision all working for you.

This is the basis you can use in 'as-if' mode upon which to build realities that you've not yet experienced – at least, not out there in the world. They will need practice to make them part of your everyday experience, but the beginning is an act of your imagination.

Now experiment with this process in another way. Think of something that you want to be able to do better than you can at the moment. Maybe it's getting your horse to step effortlessly into canter, on the correct lead, when you ask. Maybe it's sitting smoothly and adhesively to the trot. Think of any idea that helps you to distil the essence of what you're after. Maybe it's the action of striking a match that could become a shorthand for the crisp, immediate ignition you want for your canter. Maybe it's the sensation of balancing easily to the varied movements of a bus, or the Tube, that can serve to remind you that you've got the balance, the elasticity and the ability to accommodate external movement that you need for sitting trot... Take all the best bits of relevant experience that you've ever had personally, or seen in someone else. See, feel, create the experience in the virtual reality of your own mind. Replay it, perhaps several times. Notice as much detail about it as you can. A famous experiment concerning basketball players showed that a group who regularly 'practised' shooting at the net in their heads improved their performance as much as another group who actually practised on the court. The internal 'reality' of practice shaped the external reality. When you next ride, repeat your internal process briefly – then do it for real. Notice the difference your internal work has made.

Internal rehearsal like this creates and habituates neural pathways in your brain, which literally makes things happen faster, more smoothly and more naturally.

WHEN I WAS LEARNING to play the guitar years ago, I used to practise chord changes in my head before starting practice with the guitar itself – and I was amazed at how effective this was in helping my fingers to move quickly and smoothly from one position to another.

My friend Marisian, who is also one of my case-studies, practises schooling horses in her head. She finds that replaying past schooling gives her essential information about why things went as they did, and rehearsing schooling in advance gives her a way to experiment with different strategies and get them fluent before she tries them on her ponies.

Tips for Setting up an 'As-if' Frame

- Ask yourself 'what if...?' and 'how would it be if...?'

- Play 'let's imagine'.

- Let yourself just wonder...

- Do something with your horse 'as-if' you were someone you know who has a different approach, or does it better.

- Do something 'as-if' you were in another role or context from your life, or from a lifestyle you know well. What would it be like to do a long distance ride like a top secretary or senior manager? To deal with your excited horse like a primary school teacher? To manage your family, your job and your time at the yard like an international executive? This kind of 'as-if' framing is really drawing on the complex equivalents you have for each role. Each of them will have its advantages and disadvantages, just like your 'real' role – but knowing that you can draw on a range of possible 'as-ifs' gives you more options and more varied outcomes.

Like a primary school teacher...Going with the flow and attempting to harness all that energy. I am using an exaggerated blowing breath which seems to have caught Lolly's attention.

Opening up Resourcefulness

Coaching starts from the assumption that people are resourceful – usually, far more resourceful than they realize. And that goes for horses, too. Within the limits of build, age and athleticism, most of us can do better than we dare to imagine – once we allow ourselves to wonder just how good we can be. And even those apparently 'fixed' limits aren't that fixed, either. A while ago, I was judging an unaffiliated dressage competition. One horse seemed to have a great deal of potential – lovely energy and scopy movement – but was rather fresh and tense. I thought he was probably a youngster, just needing more experience and more calming. When I said as much to the competition organizer as she collected the sheets, she said: 'Do you know how old that horse is?' He was thirty!

When you put yourself into a curiosity or an 'as-if' frame of mind, you give yourself the best chance of opening up possibilities for wonder, for information and for growth, and you free yourself from many of the constraints that can limit your riding through the interconnecting mental/physical/emotional systems of which you're made. And when you open up your personal definitions of 'success', 'good' riding and other complex equivalents by finding out what they really involve for you – and then ask yourself if that's what you really want them to involve – you will be doing for yourself what a coach does: freeing yourself to discover your unique potential, and to make it real in ways you may never have dreamt were possible.

Framing in Action – Working with Jo and Nikki G

I would like to illustrate the effects of framing and reframing by looking briefly at two working sessions with my friends Jo and Nikki.

Jo used to keep her horse, Drammie (The Dramatist), at our yard. Drammie is beginning to work at Advanced level, and Jo is a stylish and experienced rider. Yet when I asked her what she'd like to achieve, she said she'd like to 'stop perching' on his back. 'Perching' seems to be a description, but it's actually a complex equivalent, and I needed to know what Jo meant by it. I also needed to know what she wanted to do instead. When you work with someone else, it's really important to find out what *they* mean by something, not what *you think* they mean; and I was interested to discover that Jo couldn't find a single word to identify what she wanted to do instead of 'perching'. She was framing her goal in 'away from' terms.

If you find that, like Jo, you're clear about what you *don't* want and not clear about what you do want, it may be because you tend towards the 'away from' end of that particular meta-programme. On the other hand, it may be simply that, because you're so focused on the thing that's giving you a problem, you haven't formulated what you *do* want very clearly. However, knowing what you do want is a really essential part of the coaching process, because how else can you shape what you want to achieve and know when you've achieved it?

I needed to find out if Jo did have a way of knowing what she wanted, even if she wasn't able to represent it clearly in words. I said that, since I didn't know exactly what she meant by 'perching' and 'not perching', I'd like her to ride round me in a circle and show me what she meant. And what Jo did without any effort was to show me two very different kinds of seat (see photos). She knew unconsciously exactly how she 'did' perching – and how to do 'not perching'. And even though she thought she couldn't ride in a non-perching

below left
Jo's ' perching' seat. She is collapsing in the waist, with no tone in her arms or legs. Drammie is active but he, too, is lacking in purpose and tone.

below right
Jo's 'not perching' seat. She is now tall through the waist, with more weight in her heels, and Drammie is able to 'rise up' in front of her.

way, she could. Because I had asked her to show me the difference, Jo accessed a complex range of stored mind-body information and translated it into action – there and then. She was more amazed than I was!

Thinking about this now, I believe that my question put Jo into an 'as-if' frame – something like saying: 'Well, I believe you when you say you can't do this, but if you could, what would it be like?' We didn't need to know how she came by the information she accessed, or why she hadn't been able to use it before. All we needed was to connect with it – and an 'as-if' frame is a great connector.

Some time ago I was working with my friend Nikki. We often swap lessons and teach each other, and on this occasion she was riding first my horse, Lolly, and then her own horse, Merlin. As we began with Lolly, I asked Nikki to tell me how he was going, and she said that he was 'mellow, but not going as forward as he sometimes does'. Hearing that she was making a mental comparison between Lolly's performance now and on other occasions when she had ridden him, I asked her to think of the best walk he had ever given her – and within seconds his walk had become more active and purposeful. We were so struck by the difference that had resulted from 'simply thinking', that we repeated the process when Nikki got on Merlin. And again, 'just thinking' brought about clear and visible differences in the horse.

This is another example of the effect of internal processing in an 'as-if' frame. When I asked Nikki to think about Lolly and Merlin giving their best walk, or best trot, connecting with the memories caused Nikki herself to behave 'as-if' the horse were offering that quality of movement there and then.

This example shows how you can use a memory of a real experience to set up your 'as-if' frame for now. But, as in Jo's case, you can also access information you may not realize you have – whether it's come from an occasional experience that you may not have registered at the time, or from indirect sources like observing others. As in these examples, behaving 'as-if' can often allow you to bypass limiting habits and assumptions and tap into new and exciting possibilities.

Finally, an example of framing at its most natural and subtle – in this case a piece of 'pairs work' between Nikki and myself. Just before completing this text, Leo and I had been picking sloes near the yard on our way home from a judging engagement, and returned to find Nikki and Beamish in the school with Nikki's husband, Mick, as attendant photographer. Having not ridden Beamish for several months, I was struck by how much lighter and more supple he looked, and said: 'I'd really like to sit on him again some time'. Immediately, Nikki replied, 'Why not have a play on him now?' I was wearing ordinary trousers and trainers, but that didn't seem to matter at all because even this briefest of permissive exchanges had got me really wanting to discover what Beamish would feel like.

My phrase 'sit on him' had reflected the neutral curiosity frame I was thinking in – and Nikki had promptly trumped me and led me towards other, even more exciting, possibilities by responding 'why not have a play on him?' Neither of us was consciously trying to 'set things up' – but that was what we were effectively doing. And the results we got show just how powerfully enabling such exchanges can be.

above Feeling our way towards lightness and harmony together.

'Look – no hands!' The delight of discovering that this perfect halt was sustained on the seat, not the rein.

8

Getting it into Words

WORDS ARE THE KEY to your mind. They are the L of NLP: Neuro-**Linguistic** Programming, and a way into the coding of the neural patterns that are held in the pathways of your brain and body, that make you the unique person that you are.

That's why language is so important. It's through language that we symbolize objects and experiences. Language stands in for experience: it's a translation medium that's essential to us in managing, sifting, coding, recalling and combining the raw data of our experience, both external (objects and events out there in the world) and internal (processes and sensations in our minds and bodies). And as I showed in the previous chapter, when explaining the importance of complex equivalents, the language each of us uses is subtly different in the richness of its meanings from the meanings that other people may attach to it. Hence the ambiguities and confusions that can arise!

So why is language important for riding, which is a physical skill? *Or is it?* Here are three key reasons:

1. The language you use tells you how you currently code and frame your experience (and how others do theirs). In particular, it reveals your characteristic ways of processing experience (your favoured representational systems).

2. Through language, you and others can choose to call up emotional states and physical behaviours in ways that help or improve your riding skills

3. If you want to enhance or to change the way you experience things, language is a great tool for leverage. Change the language, and you change the experience.

As language users, we have been using our skills in these ways, often unconsciously, all our lives. Bringing these processes into our conscious awareness, and examining them under the microscope of NLP, gives us more information – and so more power to use our existing skills more effectively and to develop them further to achieve what we really want.

Your Language and Your Coding

Let's look at how your language both expresses and reveals the way you code your riding experience.

'I can just see him qualifying for the championship.'

'I feel he's ready to move up a grade now.'

'He and I are just so in tune.'

We all understand what these sentences 'mean' – or do we? The rider who sees her horse qualifying may be telling the literal truth. She does in fact create a mental image of her horse qualifying: when she thinks, she does it primarily by making pictures. The rider who *feels* her horse is ready is not only feeling the kind of work she wants in a physical sense, she's also feeling it in her head when she thinks of him, because she draws on kinesthetic (bodily) sensation to do so. And, as is often the case, she may well be 'feeling' the satisfaction emotionally, too, since what we call emotions actually involve familiar clusterings of experience, which we have learnt to recognize and label. And the rider who says that she and her horse are so *in tune* with one another is likely to be someone for whom sound is an important source of information and an important personal processing medium.

These riders were talking about different experiences, but when people talk about the same experience, the language differences stand out even more clearly.

'We don't see eye to eye.'

'We rub each other up the wrong way.'

'There's no harmony between us.'

When we hear these words, we often just translate, getting the general meaning – 'they don't get on'. But if we listen out for language clues to the *way* the person is processing, we get far richer, and more useful, information. This helps us in working with ourselves, and it helps us to understand and build more effective relationships with other people and with our horses. We can literally 'talk the same language'.

Tips for working with Yourself

● Notice what kind of language you tend to use – catch yourself when you're chatting to someone. Spot the individual words, and the phrases and metaphors, that tend to come naturally to you. Look for themes and patterns.

● Which representational systems do you seem to use most often? Visual, kinesthetic, auditory, olfactory (smell) and gustatory (taste)?

● Cross-check with yourself to confirm whether you tend, in your daily life, to pay more attention to information coming from the external world through that/those particular sensory system(s) than you do to information from your less-used systems.

● When you're thinking something, past, present or future, notice whether you're running movies, having physical experiences, or hearing soundtracks in your mind as you do so. If you want to enhance something, to make it better or richer, you can pay attention to even more detail from your favourite system, or add in information from other systems – for example by adding a sound-track, or by asking yourself how something would feel, or whether there are accompanying smells or tastes.

Tips for Working with Others

● Listen to their language and spot the patterns. Which representational systems seem to be their favourites?

● When you talk with them, use the same system yourself, which will help you to create rapport naturally so that they feel you are 'on their wave-length', or 'know how it is to be in their shoes', or 'see things from the same perspective'.

● If they use a particular metaphor to describe something, use it yourself, or stay within the same kind of imagery, when you reply. For example, if you're a trainer whose pupil is telling you that she 'feels like a sack of potatoes, the way she's flopping about' at sitting trot, you could ask her how she would feel if she were something softer, like a sack of jelly. She may well come back with another analogy that fits what she's feeling even better than this, which is great, because it means she's engaged with your implication that she could feel differently – and more appropriately – than how she does at present. If, on the other hand, you tell her she 'looks just fine', she will have to translate your attempted reassurance into her own terms, and may not engage with it at all. Alternatively, you could respond like a coach rather than a teacher, by asking her how she would like to feel instead, and follow up whatever metaphor she offers by asking what might have to happen for a sack of potatoes to be transformed in that way. This can be a really useful and exciting way to help someone make changes in their thinking that immediately switch on quite different physiological responses. The examples at the end of this chapter illustrate how this can work in practice.

Language, States and Behaviour

Language and States

A state is how you are in your mind and body at any one time, and states are very powerful in determining not just how we feel, but how we react to and approach things, and what we can achieve. We recognize this in the common phrases 'being in a state' and 'getting into the right state' about something. Language can switch on states in a flash, because it makes us access the way we've coded our experience or our understanding. Take the word '*try*'. If someone asks you to 'try to' do something, it automatically implies the possibility that you might not succeed. (This is also the case if you are telling yourself to 'try' in your internal dialogue.) 'Try' means make an attempt, put effort in. Perhaps your attempt might not work out, or your effort might not be great enough. If, on the other hand, someone tells you to do something, there's a subtly different coding. 'Try to sit deeper' rings differently from 'Sit deeper' – whether or not you already know what's involved and whether or not you can do it. And it may also feel different again if your trainer says 'I'd like you to sit deeper', and differently again if she says 'Can you sit deeper?' or 'Could you sit deeper?' If you hear these words in the middle of a lesson you'll automatically match them up with the shade of meaning they have for you and that, in turn, will switch you into a state that corresponds, for you, with that meaning.

> Below, I've listed a range of phrases about sitting deeper. Take a few moments now to imagine yourself hearing them in the context of having a riding lesson. How does each make you feel? Notice any changes in your physiology as well as your emotional responses. You might find it useful to jot down your immediate reactions as you go along, so that you can reflect on them afterwards.

Try to sit deeper

Sit deeper

I'd like you to sit deeper

Could you sit deeper?

Can you sit deeper?

What happens if you sit deeper?

How did you react? Which phrasings would be helpful to you in your lesson? Which formulae might help you to get into the right state to sit deeper?

Monitoring not just your emotional response, but how your physiology reacts, gives you a double-check on how the words affect your state. You might be thinking 'Well, that's not quite right for me, but I know what my trainer really means and that's OK', while your body is feeling a degree of tension or unease. Registering both kinds of information, as in this case, allows you to recognize that, while you may accept a statement on one level, you may be worried, upset, irritated or angry on another. Or you may be feeling elated, cheered up, reassured – even though you thought what was said was pretty obvious or everyday. In either case, the language got to you – even though you didn't realize it immediately at a conscious level.

Furthermore, because you're riding at the time you hear the statement, it's your physiology, not your intellect, which will be communicating with your horse. If you feel your trainer is implying that you can't do something, and you feel upset about this, it's your upset that the horse will feel. If you are angry, he will feel your anger. Because he doesn't think as we do, he just responds to the messages he receives – he doesn't analyse them and say to himself: 'She isn't upset about something I'm doing, or angry with me'. He reacts to what he experiences as a message from you, which is why your 'bad days' tend to become his bad days too.

All the experienced riders I've talked to, and all the eminent equestrian writers I've read, emphasize that we need to come to riding without bringing our emotional baggage along. And that means learning how to manage our states, as I will go on to explore in Chapter 10. Knowing that the language of the mind (which, in the broadest sense, includes the 'languages' of pictures, sounds, and feelings as well as words) is enormously influential for triggering and changing states, gives us an important tool which we can work with every day.

Language and the Body

When discussing the 'as-if' frame, I mentioned that NLP and coaching both take a holistic, or systemic, approach. That is, they are based on the assumption that human beings are made up of interconnecting systems, which mutually influence and regulate each other in an almost infinite variety of ways. This is a useful assumption in practice, and one for which there is increasing scientific evidence as we accumulate detailed knowledge about the chemistry and molecular biology of the body-mind.

So far as we're concerned as riders, there's a major – and very exciting – consequence of accepting and working with this assumption. It's that, in addition to giving our bodies 'instructions', we can also access and control our physiology through mental processing of very elegant and subtle kinds.

In recent years, writers and teachers of riding have begun to make use of imagery as a way of helping riders to get their bodies to do what's wanted. *'Sit up tall like a tree and reach down with your legs like its roots reaching down into the soil'* is an example that I remember. For some riders, thinking of a tree may be exactly what they need to help them access the straightness and stretch that their trainer is after. But, precisely because it's just right for one rider, it must also stand a chance of being wrong for others.

> Take a moment. How do you respond to this image of tallness and straightness on your horse?

Perhaps you find the tree image helpful; or perhaps it irritates you. Maybe you don't think in this kind of image at all.

How *do* you think of tallness and straightness on your horse?

Perhaps you prefer to think of yourself like a ruler, or a pile of building blocks balancing on each other. Perhaps you imagine a string pulling upwards from the top of your head (an example I remember from my Alexander teacher). Maybe you like to think of pushing upwards like a bud seeking the light. Some verbalizations will switch you off; some you may be able to use if you make the effort; but the best of all will be the ones that come most naturally to you. Teach these to your trainer, or any friend trying to help you from the ground, so that they can help remind you, in your words and your way.

You can also use words in other ways to access the physiology you want, as I helped Nikki do when we were working on her posture. For her, good posture was a by-product of allowing her horse 'to be a horse and to carry her forward'. It related to her other-referenced meta-programming. We had tried images for straightness, and we had tried kinesthetic ideas like that of having a button between her shoulder-blades which was the control point. Yet it turned out that she could do what was needed for the sake of her horse more easily than

Tall and straight for the sake of the horse. Nikki and Beamish.

she could for herself. Reminding herself that she ought to sit more upright had only worked briefly when she remembered, but just thinking about allowing him to be a horse produced the upright posture and allowing seat she needed. In the fuller example at the end of this chapter, I'll show how we experimented with other approaches to the same problem, and how Nikki was able to help me in a similar way.

Experimentation and curiosity about how language affects the workings of your own body-mind are the best way forward. Become a detective, investigating your own nature and your own ways of processing. Experiment to discover what changes cause what effects. Find out what works. You'll know when you've found it, because it works instantly – just as the body-mind does. Remember that you have had a lifetime of building your own repertoire of language, coding and responding. The more you know about how you do this, the more you can harness your own processes to help you.

Change the Language, Change the Experience

Equally, you can use what you know to help you make changes where your current feelings or behaviour aren't what you'd like. You don't have to be stuck with your own patterning, however long you've done it that way, if you really don't want to any more. Telling yourself off for a feeling or behaviour you don't like or find limiting isn't enough – after all, if it were you'd have changed it by now. Telling yourself what you ought to do rarely works, either: it may just make you feel like a rebellious child being ordered about – even if you yourself are the one doing the ordering! Our internal discussions frequently involve dynamic interactions between different parts of ourselves, which can be cooperative, irritable, harmonious or confusing in just the same way as our relationships with people other than ourselves.

You will have many, if not most, of the physical capabilities you need for riding effectively, in that the human body can hold itself, bend, turn, stretch and apply its muscles in the appropriate ways. You may need to develop flexibility, strength and muscle tone, and you may be advantaged or disadvantaged by your build, physique, degree of fitness and age. But whatever your 'rider capital', you can make more of it if you use your mind, and your mind-body channels, effectively. And that means becoming a more effective user of your own language.

One way to do this is to explore different words that carry apparently similar meanings, which are actually subtly different. How does it feel, for example, to change the words '*have to*' for '*need to*' or '*want to*'? Having to muck out may not be quite the same as needing to – it's got more of a sense of compulsion in it. Even if there is no possibility of your avoiding the action itself, how would you rather think of it – even in the privacy of your own head? What's the difference between a *task*, a *challenge* and an *opportunity* – when the proposed action is exactly the same?

Another way is to listen with attentive ears to the metaphors and phrases that you and others use so often that their freshness has been lost. These 'dead metaphors' still carry their original meaning, but familiarity means that we don't hear it at a conscious level. However, we certainly do hear it unconsciously, so the power of the words can slip past your guard and affect you just the same.

> **W**HEN I FIRST MET Nicky to start our case-study work, I noticed that both she and her sister used the phrase 'take the test' to describe competing at dressage, whereas many, if not most, riders talk about 'riding the test' or 'doing the test'. 'Taking a test' usually refers to things like academic exams and driving tests, and I wondered whether, for them, the phrase reflected similar feelings about doing dressage tests. More importantly, if it did, was that how they wanted to think about dressage? If not, every time they used the phrase they would inadvertently be reinforcing meanings and associations they might not want dressage competitions to have.

Weasel Words

When we think of the power of words and put that together with a coaching approach, we see the possibility of some very refined influence and interventions. This applies whether you're thinking of how you coach yourself, how your trainer teaches you, or how you seek to teach and help others. In a chapter that's concerned with the power of language, I want now to consider what I think of as 'weasel words' – the small, subtle, purposeful hunters of the language world. I'm going to explore just a few of these to show how they can affect you in a flash and limit, or enhance, what you do – and I'm sure you'll be able to think of others that have the same kind of power, whether for you as a unique individual, or more generally for you and other people you know.

If you can train yourself to notice them, you'll increasingly be able to avoid what I call the *killers*, and to take advantage of those I've called the *trackers* because they help you to keep on track for what you want.

Killer Weasels

But (and though, and apart from)

These negate what comes just before them. Even if you don't notice at the time, they can be a powerful means of undermining or cancelling what went before.

'Your seat is really improving, *apart from when he's playing you up.*'

'I really enjoy jumping – *though not big fences.*'

'Let yourself flow with the movement *but remember to keep your elbows in.*'

Try

As I explained earlier in this chapter, 'try' always implies the possibility of failure, whether someone is asking you to 'try to' do something or you're saying 'I'll try to do…' to yourself or someone else. Either you'll do it, or not. If you do it, you've succeeded. Maybe you could do it better, but that's another issue. And if someone asks you to 'try to', they're really giving you a disguised command and at the same time implying that you may not be able to manage what they're asking. If you want to test out the effect, just consider how differently you might feel if your teacher asked you to 'have a go at…' or 'see what happens if you do…'. These are both permissions to experiment, whereas 'try to' implies you have to succeed or else…you'll feel a fool/you'll know how bad you are/she'll think you haven't got what it takes, etc.).

Just

This is a word that attempts to minimize, and to disguise the minimizing! '*I'll just* brush him down before I give you a hand with the feeds' probably means, in fact, that you'll have finished by the time the last feed has been delivered – but you'll have had both the credit for offering to help and at the same time a legitimate reason for not managing to do it. '*I'll just* make that quick phone call while you're getting him ready' probably means that you'll be late for the start of your pupil's lesson. In dealing with this particular weasel, drop the 'just' out to get the true meaning. If you do that before you utter the words, you may have time to rethink what you're really saying; and if you delete it from what someone else is telling you, you can make a better estimate of what they're really saying, and call their bluff if you need to or want to.

Only

'I'm only a happy hacker.'

'I'm only a novice.'

'I've only got this to do before I can do that.'

'Only' is a minimizer and often a put-down, which undervalues what it applies to. *'Only a happy hacker'* may be an indirect defence, implying that you know the other person thinks hacking is just playing about and not serious riding, but you want to do it anyway and not have a row about it, so you appear to agree with what you think are their values. *'Only a novice'* lets you off a similar hook, because it implies that people shouldn't expect too much of you. *'Only having this to do'* means that you *have* got to do it, and that you think/hope it won't take up too much time. How is it different if you say 'I can do that after I've done this'?

'He's only a pony'... So...?

Marisian and Charlie.

Can't

'I can't do sitting trot without stirrups.'

'Can't' is a word that stands in for many shades of meaning, and often it's good to explore which one is really involved. Literally, 'can't' is a shortened form of 'cannot'. So the first question it begs is: 'What stops you?' Is it lack of knowledge, or lack of skill, or perhaps fear of some kind? Often, when you ask yourself if you truly cannot do something, you find that the answer is 'No'. In that case, try substituting one of these instead:

'I won't do sitting trot without stirrups because...'

'I don't want to do sitting trot without stirrups because...'

'I choose not to do sitting trot without stirrups because...'

You'll probably know at once if one of these comes closer to your true meaning – and, if so, you will have more information to work with.

Lazy (and other negative complex equivalents)

Lazy is a very commonly used word, and because it's an abstract label it's a complex equivalent. So the first point about it is that it can mean different things to different people. But it also carries quite a negative charge, so it can dishearten you or condemn your horse even when you don't know exactly what it means!

A good way of dealing with this kind of weasel word is to ask yourself what exactly is someone doing or not doing to earn this description, and who is concerned about that – and why? Usually, the word reveals more about the speaker's hopes or intentions or values than anything else.

'He's a lazy horse' can mean 'He didn't do what I wanted', or 'He isn't naturally forward', or 'He's not in front of my leg', or 'He wasn't paying attention'. In other words, his behaviour tells you something about his response to *you* – and, beyond that, it tells you that you're disappointed, angry or frustrated because you haven't been able to get the response you wanted. In NLP terms, 'lazy' actually tells you that you've not found a way of getting your message across. So, when you think your horse is lazy, the question to ask is how can you make it worth his while to do what you want – in other words, how can you motivate him. And if you're using the word about yourself, as in *'I'm too lazy to school every day'*, ask yourself what would need to happen for you to feel really motivated and excited about schooling. Whereas the word 'lazy', like many negative complex equivalents, closes investigation down, searching for the missing motivation is often very fruitful. You're looking at a formula that goes like this: what would have to happen for [the opposite of the complex equivalent] to be the case? And that gives you ideas that can take you forward.

What-if?

'What-if?' has a foot in both camps. It can be either a killer or (as we shall see shortly) a tracker, because it engages you in what follows. It's an invitation to imagine and, as we know, what you imagine with intensity and corroborative detail is internally as real, at the time, as 'out-there' reality – and can therefore affect you almost as much. 'What-if?' is a killer if it starts you imagining disaster scenarios – *'What if he bucks and I fall off?'* In such a case, stop the process right there by saying firmly to yourself (or anyone else who's just said it in this way): *'And what if he doesn't?'* This is the time to reason, work out probabilities, look at the evidence, get grounded again. An alternative that can also be very helpful is to stay with the 'what-if' question and ask yourself some survival questions:

'Would that be so dreadful?'

'How could I manage that situation?'

'What could I do?'

'What else could I do?'

All of these defuse the 'what-if', this time by applying reality tests in another way. They allow you to think of ways to prevent, and ways to retrieve, the situation, and to get back in charge of your mind, which has begun to run away with you. And that is actually far more disabling than the majority of realistic disasters you are likely to foresee.

Tracker Weasels

Tracker weasels are helpful for exactly the same reason that killer weasels often are not: they slip past your internal critic and get you engaged with their meaning without you even realizing it. And sometimes that can be really helpful. Cultivating tracker weasels, whether you're talking to someone else or thinking to yourself, gives you a very elegant way of shifting emphasis and suggesting new possibilities. After all, since reality is so often what you make it, why not make it to your advantage?

Yet

'I can't do sitting trot – *yet*'. Just adding this one word opens up the possibility that one day you will be able to. It allows you to shift your attention from a current inability (with the feelings that go along with it) to a future possibility – with the feelings that go along with that. 'He doesn't understand the canter aid – *yet…*' takes the edge off your frustration with your young horse as you effectively remind yourself that he's still learning.

And

'And' is a balancing and equalizing word, especially when you use it instead of 'but': 'I enjoy riding, *but* I find it hard to get enthusiastic on dark winter evenings.' Both the statements in this sentence may be true for you. Yet if you join them together with 'but' the effect is to cancel out the enjoyment because 'but' qualifies it. If you use 'and' instead ('I enjoy riding, *and* I find it hard to get enthusiastic on dark winter evenings'), the sentence as a whole may sound rather odd – yet it allows the two statements to stand as equals without modifying each other. You enjoy riding. Yes. You also find it hard to get enthusiastic on dark winter evenings – you and the rest of us! 'And' isn't emotionally loaded, so using it makes you more aware of the contrast between the potential enjoyment you have in riding and the fact that the way in which you have to do it isn't ideal. So, potentially, 'and' allows you to begin to explore more easily what you might need, or want, to do to improve things.

Wonder (and related words)

'Wonder' is a word that makes you search for meaning, and 'search-words' are great because they get you opening up, investigating, pondering, asking yourself questions. *Wondering why* gets you thinking about cause. *Wondering how* gets you thinking about process. *Wondering what* gets you thinking about specifics, as do *wondering who or when*. Wondering is part of curiosity framing.

Other search words with similar effects are *imagine* and *consider*. You can also convert almost any abstract word like *success, happy, achievement, disappointment, submission, elevation, swing*, and even *on the bit* into search words if you remind yourself that they flag up specifics, for you and for others – and ask yourself '*What specifics?*'

What-if?

The very words tell you that you are dealing with something imagined, not with an actual reality. So the tracker function of 'what-if' is that it leads you into a reality test:

What-if x did happen?

What-if it didn't?

You are exploring probabilities, fears and contingencies.

For example: '*What-if this youngster of mine turns out to have national (or international) potential?*'. There might be exciting consequences – or problematical ones. If he's that good, do you have the skill to match his development? Can you afford the training, competition and travelling costs? Would you feel justified in keeping him at home and only riding him for pleasure? Would you be disappointed if his early promise didn't blossom further? What-if…? Use the words as a clue that there is more for you to explore and to ground in real, everyday terms.

Thus we can say that when they lead on to unrealistic fantasizing, even apparently positive 'what-ifs' are of little value to you – and the quick test is exactly the same as for negative ones. 'What-if I don't (win the Lottery)?' is your helpful dose of cold water. But encouraging yourself to imagine positive 'what-ifs' is one key way of changing the scope of your dreams – so long as you then bring your Realist and Critic in to help you. (See Chapter 9 for an outline of this strategy.)

As; While

These two have similar effects, in that they link what comes before with what comes after in a time relationship. 'I'll go over my test *as* I'm mucking out'. 'Why don't we plan our training programme *while* we're out hacking today?' These statements are pretty straightforward, in that they only refer to things happening at the same time as each other. But you can load the same linking words with a different kind of emphasis.

'*While I'm warming up I'll notice what he's giving me and think about what I want to focus on today.*'

'*As we practise making the canter circles smaller and larger again I'll be thinking about how canter pirouettes felt on that schoolmaster I used to ride.*'

Going back to the earlier example, discussing training strategies while on a hack may be useful but isn't adding definite value to the present or the future. In these latter examples, however, you're choosing to link an ongoing activity with another that can draw from it and build on it. You're gaining more from what you're actually doing by making it link with a purpose that relates directly to it. You're getting twice the value.

In this chapter I've explored some of the many ways in which you can use language to help yourself and other riders find out more about what works; to access the physiology you want subtly and elegantly, to take yourself on voyages of exploration into the futures you want to create, and to make changes to what frustrates and limits you. Your language is as much a skill in your riding as your balance, your flexibility and your strength. In the examples that follow, I'm going to show how an awareness of language and its power helped Nickki and me to achieve what we wanted. And that, in turn, will lead on to the important issue of outcomes.

Words in Action – Wendy and Nikki G

In the previous chapter I pointed out a number of ways in which words can influence us as riders, and I want to illustrate this from two of the coaching sessions that Nikki and I regularly exchange with each other. Sometimes we swop horses as well as trading support, but on these occasions we were each riding our own.

Wendy and Lolly

I had been building up my riding fitness following a major operation, and had been concentrating on my own flexibility and strength at the same time as getting reacquainted with Lolly, whom I've ridden much less often than Vals during the last few years. So I had a broad agenda for this session – one which focused on my needs rather than on Lolly's schooling – and I was mostly doing rising trot and canter rather than making heavier demands on my stomach muscles through attempting sitting trot.

I assume that Nikki felt I was being a little stiff, because after a while she asked me to imagine that Lolly and I were not in the school, but out for a hack. 'Imagine it's a lovely, bright autumn morning and you're cantering over an open stubble field together...', she said. Lolly and I used to hack every Wednesday – it was our day off together and our treat, and we greatly enjoyed playing hookey from dressage. I don't think that he and I have actually cantered together over stubble fields, but I've certainly walked and ridden over them. However, it wasn't necessary for me to have actually had that experience, because Nikki's words, and the tone of her voice, first engaged my imagination and then trailed off at just the right moment so that I could immerse myself in what she had helped me to create. And that was enough to make an astonishing difference. As I thought of that big, open space and the generously enthusiastic canter Lolly produces when he's enjoying himself hacking, that's exactly what he produced in the school. We were there and not there. And I 'did' nothing to make it happen, other than enter that experience in my head.

I can explain this just as I did in the previous chapter: the words engaged my internal experience, and that brought about subtle differences in my physiology through the mind-body connection, and so Lolly felt the permission and the encouragement and responded with big, rhythmical, enthusiastic, ground-covering strides. Although I knew exactly what Nikki was after – and what she was doing to achieve it – it worked just the same, because she was working with me, alongside me, and for my enjoyment and that of my horse. And it was a miracle and a mystery, even though every bit of it was open and understandable.

This was great coaching because it enabled rider and horse to discover more of what they were capable of, in an entirely permissive way. As Gallwey suggests, it opened our minds to what was observable, relevant and interesting. And because of all of those factors, it was effortless and fun. There was an additional lesson for me, too: if I could achieve this in the school, I could achieve it anywhere else – in a dressage test, for example, or across country. The words allowed me to tap into my stored experience and thus transform the reality of actual events. And they could again – because once something has been discovered it becomes a resource that can be drawn on deliberately when wanted or needed.

Nikki and Beamish

NLP offers us many such miracles, because it gives us access to the miracles of our minds. Even so, it's important to recognize that some things will call for a range of experiments or approaches, and may tax our self-knowledge and resourcefulness. Nikki's pattern of looking down is an example of this. Over the years we've been working together, we've tried a number of approaches, each of which has been helpful to an extent. Defocusing helped, because it encouraged her to look ahead rather than down. Thinking of the space between her shoulder-blades as if there were a button there helped her shoulder-blades to flatten and her chest to become more open. Imagining that she was showing her horse's abilities to a watching audience helped, because Nikki tends to be other-referenced and found it easier to ride proudly on his behalf rather than her own. But here she was again, riding round and looking down.

My first idea was to engage her imagination as she'd done mine. 'If you were hacking', I said, 'you'd need to look watch out for things ahead of you. There might be a pheasant in that hedge, or a gate to aim for...' This helped – for a bit, when she remembered. But the old droop came back. This time I took a different coaching approach, because clearly something was maintaining the old pattern at a more significant level. Nikki's stance and expression both told me that she was in a serious, inward-focused state – one which wasn't giving her much joy at that moment and which was making her position less effective than it can be.

It was time for a search question to test what I thought I was seeing.

'What kind of a state are you in when you're riding like that? You look quite serious and inward, to me...'

As I'd hoped, this sent Nikki off inside herself to check out what I had said. 'I suppose I'm in a trying state...', she said. I have talked about trying states earlier in this book, and shown how they can interfere with our potential. And Nikki and I had recognized in our work together that 'trying' inhibits her and often blocks both her investigative ability and her fluency as a rider.

'And what kind of state do you *want* to be in?' I asked.

'An experimenting state. A curiosity state. A playful state – yes, a playful state.'

And with this, Nikki's physiology changed. She became more upright and more relaxed. And so Beamish also relaxed, and together they were able to spend the rest of the session experimenting with ways of achieving the balance, flexibility, lightness and enjoyment of their own movement that is the next step forward for them both.

As I've tried to show, language is an important key to developing our riding experience in the ways that we want, and through the mind-body connection it can help us to make instant and effortless changes. Effective riders and good trainers instinctively use it in these ways, and achieve similar results. Yet it's

An experimenting
state. A curiosity state.
A playful state. Nikki
and Beamish.

important for us to recognize that working with language, like every other
strategy that NLP has helped us identify, is one of many approaches, each of
which may make 'the difference that makes a difference'. We need to keep
experimenting and playing with these wonderful tools – all the time – because
riding is an activity that's never completed, but always in process. It's always in
need of refining – and, indeed, that's half the fun of it.

PART **3**

Groundwork

9

Getting What You Really Want

So FAR, WE'VE LOOKED AT some of the distinctive ways in which coaching can help you make the most of your riding. You've become alert to what your observation tells you, and to the contribution each of your senses has to make. You have a tool for knowing where you are and measuring your progress. You know how you and your horse tick as unique creatures in conversation with each other, and what your meta-programme patterning means in terms of strengths and limitations. You know about different kinds of framing, and where each tends to lead you. And you know about the leverage of language.

But what do you want from your riding?

Think again. What do you *really, really* want?

In this chapter, I'm going to show you how coaching can help you to clarify your answers to these two questions – and the answers to each may not necessarily be the same. Adding the *really, really* part tends to focus us on deeper, perhaps less recognized goals than those which come up as a first response. After all, you want to improve your riding. Yes? You want your horse to go better. Yes? Do you want to *enjoy* your riding? Well, that as well. Or perhaps have fun with your horse? That, too. To discover more about your body, how it behaves and how you can control it better? That might be interesting. To overcome some of your anxieties and limitations, to feel more confident, become more assertive? Great – but how can riding help with things like that?

Becoming your own riding coach can, indeed, help you achieve all these things, because when you ride you aren't a different person from the person you are at home, or at work, or among your friends. You are a whole person, and when you take a coaching approach to your feelings, thoughts and behaviour, the patterns you observe in one area of your life and the adjustments you make to them will spill over into the other areas. There is plenty of evidence to demonstrate the truth of this amongst the case-study riders featured in this book. As Nicky M increased her independence and discovered enjoyment in experimenting as a rider, she found herself becoming more confident and assertive at work and in her close relationships. As Nikki G began to own her skill and feel pride in what she and her horse could do, she became more confident as a teacher – and, to the envy of her friends, her skiing also improved! And as Sean became engrossed in discussions with his strongly differing horses, he started to think of himself as a dressage rider, not just as an eventer doing dressage.

Changes like these can affect us on any one or more of the logical levels, from apparently simple changes in environment and behaviour, right through to important shifts of emphasis in identity.

A dressage rider, not just an eventer doing dressage. Sean with Kluedo at the Winter Finals.

Exploring your riding with curiosity and commitment is likely to bring you more than you anticipate. So it's worthwhile having a good look at your goals, and finding out what you really, really want: with this framework, you're likely to get it.

NLP and coaching have given us some powerful tools to work with in this respect, and I'm going to show you how they can work for you.

First, you need to know what you do really, really want.

Second, you may need some help both in 'thinking outside the box' about what you want and about how to deal with current obstacles, blocks and limitations. Robert Dilts, one of the most influential developers of NLP right from its early days, identified three key roles that are involved in thinking and behaving creatively – and it's creativity that we need to open up our horizons. These roles are those of **dreamer**, **realist** and **critic**, and each has something to offer you in becoming you own best riding coach.

Third, there's the question of ensuring that your goals are achievable. NLP has identified a number of factors that can help you with this. Together, they make up a set of essential criteria against which you can test your goal to ensure that you will be giving it the best chance of success.

Fourth, however much you want something, however achievable it is, you need a way to relate today's schooling – and tomorrow's – to it, to ensure that you keep on track. You need to be able to break down a larger goal into smaller, achievable steps (the chunking down process described in Chapter 5) and you need to audit, review and plan ahead. You also need to be able to improvise with inspiration and confidence, trusting yourself to respond to what happens on the day, even if it is not what you had planned, and adapting your approach to ensure that the way you deal with it takes you just as surely towards your goal as the plan you'd first thought of, and perhaps had to abandon. If you keep your long-term goal in mind (which is chunking up), you will still be working towards it, even though in a different way. You need the confidence to think on your feet, and the firm sense of purpose to ensure that your thinking takes you in the right direction.

Fifth, these close-up, hands-on skills need to be linked all the time to a clear sense that you and no one else owns your riding. Not your horse, though you need to discuss things with him at every stage. Not your trainer, though her expertise and encouragement can be invaluable. Not your horsy friends, partner, family, or disciplinary body, however much you value their input and their support. If someone else owns your riding, there will always be a part of you that is shut off, held back, kept in reserve. Whatever kind of riding you're doing, however little or often, whether you're ambitious or ride 'just for fun', you want your involvement, your learning and your enjoyment to be whole-hearted – even if it means sometimes that your frustration and disappointment are wholehearted too. All this means that you know *why* you're riding and what matters to you – and it may mean that you need to 'train' people around you so that they understand it, too.

What I'm offering you is a view of riding that's holistic: riding as an expression of what it means to you to be alive. If that sounds grandiose, just pause to think about the best – and the worst – riding moments you've experienced. My guess is that, like the great riders whose words have come down to us in their writings, your riding is a reflection of what matters to you in life. That's why you bother to read books about it. It's important. It's the same for me. A coach respects and takes very seriously anything that's important to the person they're working with. Let's explore what some of that respectful concern means in action, when you are coaching yourself.

What do You Really, Really Want?

The key here is honesty – first of all with yourself, and then with others. Remember that conversations between a coach and the person being coached are confidential – and also that sometimes it's difficult to disclose your true thoughts and feelings, even to a sympathetic person who's on your side. You may need to work quite hard to be on *your own* side sometimes.

When we started as a family to ride dressage, people around us automatically expected that we would want to compete. Other people at the yard went off to shows at weekends; our trainer had always been involved in competitions, whether showing, carriage driving, jumping or doing dressage. Of course we would compete! My husband Leo and daughter Charlotte quite liked competing. I hated it. I thought it was because I was nervous – well, I was. I thought it was because I wasn't confident that my riding was good enough (it wasn't). However, it has taken me years – and a lot of NLP training – to recognize that I don't like competition in any area of my life, and that that's all right.

That's an 'away from'. When I first recognized it, all sorts of discussions went on in my head. Perhaps I should make myself compete – if I found it difficult it might be 'good for me'. Since I was a judge (no problems there, after a lifetime of teaching and observing people), perhaps I owed it to the competitors I judged to put myself in the same boat. My internal dialogue produced internal conflict – and most of these thoughts were based on theories or 'oughts', not on any established 'truths'.

Once I swept this kind of clutter out of my thinking, I became a lot clearer. Once I asked myself what I really, really want (and have always really, really wanted,) I got a direct, simple answer. I want to enjoy my riding. I want to get better at it, and work to improve it as long as I am physically able to. I want to have better, simpler and more effective conversations with any horse I ride. I'm happy to learn from others, in a coaching context. I'm happy to monitor and question myself. None of these things involves competition. Knowing this means that I can enjoy my riding, work rigorously towards my real goals, and stop hassling myself – and this makes it easier for me to keep to my agenda, rather than unintentionally falling in with other people's. It also means that I can explain my aims more effectively to people helping with my training.

Internal dialogues of the 'ought', 'must' and 'should' kind usually involve imagining what other people might think – and, especially, how they might be judging you. In NLP and coaching, we try to avoid 'mind-reading' because it's based on fantasy, not on hard evidence. (We will be dealing with hard evidence later on.)

So that's why the *really, really* part makes a difference. Often, the answer you come up with may differ substantially from the one you first thought of – or even contradict it.

 What do you really, really want from your riding?

Nowadays, no one is forced to ride. We have cars, trains and buses with which to get about. People in the past may well have had to ride even if they were fearful, or unfit, or uncoordinated. We don't. Get back to your real reasons for doing it – and respect that you have a right to them.

Thinking Outside the Box: the Dreamer, the Realist and the Critic

In his book *Tools for Dreamers*, Robert Dilts shows the extent to which creativity is needed: not just to think of new approaches (innovation), but to think of *different* approaches. We need creativity most of all when we're stuck, because it can help us get away from our tramlined thinking and change our repetitive patterns of behaviour. In terms of riding, we don't need to invent new ways of doing things – it really is the case that most strategies for dealing with horses have been thought of by now. Classical riding is just that – classical both in the sense that it was developed in the periods we think of as classical, and classical in the other sense that we revere its methods for their elegance and streamlined appropriateness for the tasks in hand.

Where we do need creativity is in the application of skill and strategy to specific situations. We need a knowledge base that gives us choices: that we can learn through lessons, books, videos, etc. And in order to make effective choices we need to experiment, and to evaluate the effectiveness of our experiments. At the end of this chapter I will show how this kind of creative thinking can help rider and horse as they work together.

The early developers of NLP noticed that the people who were most influential in any situation were the ones with the greatest variety of possible responses. One of the skills they frequently called upon was their ability to change their perspective on things. Stepping into someone else's shoes (taking second position), and viewing a situation as if they were an observer, even when they were actually involved themselves (taking third position), meant that they weren't just stuck with how they thought and felt in their own first position.

When Dilts was trying to find out about the structure of creativity, someone who worked with Walt Disney told him that you never knew which Disney was going to come into the room: sometimes he would be a dreamer, sometimes a realist and sometimes a critic. Dilts then developed the use of these roles as a deliberate strategy to help people become more creative and to test that what they came up with was viable in practice.

Let's consider how taking these three roles can help you become more effective in your riding. It's very easy to step straight into Critic mode, which may mean making yourself feel bad or inadequate. But remember that, using this strategy, the Critic comes last – and this role isn't just negative, it is one of evaluation, so it can really help you evaluate the effectiveness of what you're doing.

Start, instead, with your Dreamer. This is the part of you that dares to wonder, and to imagine the unknown and the new. When you're in Dreamer mode, there are no rules about what you can and can't imagine. Let yourself go. Your Dreamer can help you find out what you'd really, really like – but never dared to let yourself think about before. Your Dreamer can also explore what might happen if..., playing with new strategies and wild ideas. Your Dreamer may think of fifteen different ways to help your horse learn to strike off in canter on the leg you choose... Or tell you a story that will help you remember your dressage test. Or have you riding through the wild back country of the American Rockies, or the old gold rush areas of New Zealand. The Dreamer doesn't have to be practical – though often it's the dreams that get you past practical difficulties. Einstein's Dreamer had him riding a beam of light through space, which then led to him formulating the Theory of Relativity. The dream came first. Perhaps your dream involves riding the airs above the ground... or completing Badminton... What will it be like?

Then it's time for your Realist. The Realist is about nuts and bolts – not about put-downs. It's about *how, when, where, what* might be involved in making your dream happen. What are the finances? Who could help you? What skills would you need? What steps would you need to take next? The Realist helps you with your plans, systems and the practical feasibility of your dream.

Finally it's time for the Critic. Although, in common use nowadays, the word 'critic' often is employed just to mean someone who's negative, originally the term meant someone who evaluated (as in theatre or film critic). In Dilts' creativity model, the Critic is an impartial evaluator, not a nit-picking moralizer or spoilsport. This Critic is the one who tests out the practicalities your Realist came up with, and helps you evaluate them in a wider context. Your Realist may help you plan your horse's training and carry it out so that you work effectively towards your goal. Your Critic may help you use feedback from the wider world to assess, for example, the likelihood that you'll be selected for your local team, or make it to the Horse of the Year Show. Sometimes, the result may be that you abandon an idea – but that's because the Critic has helped you to discover exactly how and why it might not work, or how it could involve you in things you hadn't foreseen – not because the Critic has undermined you and made you feel incompetent. And when your Critic looks at your competition results, feedback from your trainer and the way your horse is going and says 'Go for it!', you know that you stand a good chance – because your Critic is actually an objective assessor of hard evidence.

Take some time to think about what you want from your riding from each of these perspectives: Dreamer, Realist and Critic. Jot down the ideas that come to you at each stage. What have you learnt?

Well-formed Goals

There are six NLP criteria for checking how good a chance you stand of achieving your chosen goal. These are:

1. Is it stated positively?

If your goal is phrased negatively (e.g. you want your horse to *stop* doing something) you will not have a clear sense of purpose to aim for. Once you know what you *do* want him to do instead, you can harness your thoughts and your actions to bring this about.

2. Can you specify what you will see, hear, feel (and perhaps also taste and smell) when you achieve it?

'I want to succeed with my horse', or 'I want to have fun with my horse', or 'I want to be a good rider' all sound like reasonable goals – but what will tell you that you've achieved them? If you know what you'll be seeing, hearing and feeling, you'll have a clearer sense of how you can build up to your goal bit by bit, and a better way of benchmarking your eventual success.

3. Is the process of working towards it and achieving it within your control?

It's amazing how often we want something that isn't within our control! If you really want to work in a covered school, don't hope that you'll win the Lottery. That's not within your control. Instead, think about changing yards, hiring a school on occasion when you want to prepare for something special, finding a trainer who's based at a yard with one, saving money, selling something or extending your mortgage…

4. Do you know exactly what will be involved in achieving it?

You know what your senses will tell you when you ride that winning round – but where will you be? What series of qualifiers will take you there? Will you need extra lessons? Will you need to borrow or buy a trailer? Who will be your back-up team? Questions like these are about planning and organization, and the more you have worked these things out, the better. Professionals plan their show diaries backwards from the major events they want to succeed in: that way, they have enough shows to give them a chance of qualifying, and some to spare, and they don't have to jettison their plans if their horse throws a shoe, or pulls a muscle, or if they get hurt themselves and can't ride for a while.

5. Can you achieve it without losing anything that is currently useful, valuable or important to you?

When you're set on a goal, you may think at first that nothing would be lost if you achieved it. But often there is actually something you'd miss in how things are at the moment – and sometimes that's what's holding you back. If your ambition is to own a horse for the first time, imagine having to keep him exercised six days a week. That's fine in the summer, but what about early mornings before work, or dark winter evenings? If you enjoy a full social life, what kind of dent will a busy competition schedule make in it? Knowing what you may have to give up – or get yourself into – means that you can make good choices and thorough plans, and that you won't be surprised by what achieving your goal has let you in for.

6. Can you afford what it will cost you, in terms of money, time and your sense of who you are and what's important to you?

Doing the maths – with the help of your Realist, not your Dreamer! – means that you're less likely to be surprised, and to find yourself seriously out-of-pocket. The same is true for time – and horses always take more time than we think! The issues of your identity and your beliefs and values, get you cross-checking that your goals sit comfortably with you at really vital levels. If they don't, you're almost certain to sabotage them one way or another. In a pinch, however much we may think we want to achieve something, we won't easily compromise what matters deeply to us.

If you can answer 'yes' to all of these questions, you are more likely to achieve your goal than if any of the answers are 'no'. A 'no' answer is still very useful feedback, however, because it shows you an area where you need to become clearer, or make adjustments.

Keeping on Track (Chunking Up and Down)

An important function of coaching is that it helps you to keep on track. When someone else is coaching you, they can ask you questions, get you to review progress, and so on. When you're solo schooling, this is something you have to do for yourself. And chunking is a useful tool, because it's a way of helping you relate what's going on (or not going on) here and now to your overall aims or longer-term plans. Chunking simply means changing the volume of information you're dealing with at any one time. You could think of it as a way of changing focus by zooming in and out like a camera lens, or as alternating stepping back with getting right up close. And when you move back and forth between the big picture and the detail, you have a good means of assessing how they relate to each other.

Let's think about how this might help you in practice. If you want to take your horse on a long distance ride, you won't expect him to do the full distance without building up his strength and stamina through shorter distances first. That makes sense. But if you're planning to do a dressage test, you might think it makes sense to rehearse it from start to finish as a pattern. Often, professional riders don't do this – partly because many horses are quick learners and can learn to anticipate what comes next, rather than 'listening' for the rider's aid. Also 'going through' the whole test is a distinct aim, which you may accomplish at the cost of other aims, such as perfecting the individual movements or, indeed, the way they flow together. Thus it often makes more sense to chunk right down and work at the different components separately. Several professionals I know don't rehearse tests as entireties at all: they just remind themselves of the test and ride it on the day. That way, the horse is fresh and attentive, and the rider's focus is on what is actually happening.

There's another kind of chunking that can help us, too. Chunking sideways – in other words, looking for another version of the same thing. When Dilts is talking about creative problem solving, he calls it 'lateral chunking'. Coaching offers a simple way to put this into action. Whenever a plan or a strategy doesn't work, ask yourself the simple question *'And what else?'* As Mr Spock of *Star Trek* fame once said in a sticky spot: *'There are always alternatives'.*

Chunking will help you make each schooling session purposeful and productive. Think, as you get yourself and your horse ready, what stage he's at in his learning, and what stage the two of you are at in your partnership. How does that relate to your hopes and aims? How could you use today to work towards them?

A while ago I went to ride our old schoolmaster, Lolly. How was I going to use the time? I had been thinking about weight aids and working with Leo to help him stretch down his inside leg as a way of influencing Lolly without relying on the rein to tell him to turn. I thought that maybe I would play with this myself. Experimenting in this way would help me test how influential I could be, and increase the subtlety of the conversations Lolly and I could have together. It would also give me some more first-hand data I could draw on when coaching other riders.

So my large chunk aims were:

- to experiment

- to increase the subtlety of our conversations

- to refine a teaching tool.

The influence of stretching down. (a) Moving to the right. (b) Moving to the left. While I am remaining straight in my upper body, the level of my heels shows the stretch which is telling Lolly to move one way or the other.

What I actually did (small chunk activity) once we'd warmed up, was to play with four- and five-loop serpentines in our long school, relying on changing my weight rather than using my reins, or changing my outside leg and shoulder position, to tell Lolly what I wanted. I wasn't bothered about getting a correct bend – only interested in finding out whether we could draw the serpentine shapes. And we could.

a.   b.

Lolly is used to serpentines, and with old schoolmasters you can never rule out the influence of previous learning. No doubt there's a bit of him that thought: 'Well, she's telling me in a different way but I know about serpentines and I bet that's what she's after'. So the next chunk up was to do something he couldn't decode so easily. I turned onto the three-quarter line in trot, faced straight ahead, and then simply stretched down into one stirrup and then the other. What we got was a shallow zigzag as Lolly stepped under each of my stretched-down legs in turn.

Since we had been in discovery mode rather than a 'trying' mode, all this was fun – and the small chunk activities had also helped us to develop our (larger chunk) communication skills, exactly as I'd hoped.

Chunking is, in fact, a process that helps you be accountable to yourself. If you finish a session wondering why you did what you did, or feel that it didn't take you forward, taking a few minutes to chunk up to your wider goals will often tell you why that was, and allow you to explore what would have to happen for you to get back on track. It can be like a compass, monitoring small, as well as larger, deviations from your chosen path. And it will also help you to recognize when you've just gone down a blind alley, or got stuck. And because you have broken your large chunk goal down into smaller mini-goals, you have given yourself the possibility of lots more moments of satisfaction and achievement.

Owning Your Riding

As I have been pointing out, coaching is aimed at helping people to become clear about what they really want, finding out what steps they need to take to achieve their goals, and working towards them with commitment. It isn't always a soft option; but if you take a thinking approach to your riding you'll enjoy working with its tools, even when you're temporarily having problems.

Sometimes you may be dealing with disappointment; sometimes self-coaching may help you realize that you need to change direction. One of the side effects that people usually experience is that, through taking themselves seriously and putting systematic thought and effort into the processes involved, they become more in tune with themselves at many levels, and can express what they feel, think and want with greater clarity and confidence. In this sense, what begins as a riding-related process spreads to include much more of yourself than that. And as you get to own your riding more, you'll also be getting to own yourself in a broader sense.

Coaching is not aimed at making you more selfish, going all out for what you want at the expense of others. You can make all the compromises you choose – but you'll be aware of the choices you are making, and own them, not just drift into them. This is partly because coaching, like NLP, gets you thinking about how you are coming over to others, and what *their* experience and feelings are likely to be. Going right back to something I covered earlier, coaching involves you becoming more aware of more information. More information means the possibility of more choices. Owning yourself is, paradoxically, a way to improve how you get on with other people in your life, as well as with your horse.

If you can be clear with yourself about what you want from you riding, it becomes easier to explain it to your friends and family. It also makes it easier to tell your trainer what kind of help you need – and if your current trainer can't offer you what you want, it's then clearer for both of you that the mutually best option would be for you to find another trainer. Clarity often simplifies things for everyone involved.

This chapter has been concerned with how you find your path, get on it and stick to it. In the next chapter I'm going to look at some of the common traps solo schoolers find themselves falling into, and some of the limiting states these can produce. And I'm going to offer you a model for recognizing and managing these traps and states effectively. Paradoxically, it's a model that involves a lot of PLAY.

Goals in Action – Sean and Kluedo

Every time we ride we have the possibility of fine-tuning what we do so that it helps us towards our overall goals, and here I want to show how Sean and I were able to do this in one of our sessions together.

Sean and I had been working with Georgie, but when I arrived he told me that Georgie was ill, so we agreed that on this occasion we'd work with Kluedo, one of his other clients' horses, instead. Kluedo is lighter in build than Georgie, and more established in Medium level work. He is forward-going, but when he doesn't understand what's wanted, or finds it difficult, he tends to stop and rear.

As Sean worked him in, we discussed Kluedo's stage of training and agreed that, although his forwardness was attractive and rhythmical, in order to progress he would need to develop more self-carriage. To achieve this Sean would need to help him slow his trot and convert some of his energy into upward, elastic movement rather than allowing him to cover so much ground. This would provide a more secure basis for advanced movements as his training developed.

We realized that Kluedo might find it difficult to engage and carry himself more, in part because he has a longish back, so we agreed that the new work would need to be built up gradually and in short bursts. As soon as Sean asked for the slower, more cadenced trot, Kluedo did a few strides, then stopped, stuck his head out and forward to disengage over his back, and began his rearing pattern. This pattern repeated each time that Sean asked – several times in all. Kluedo understood what was wanted, and was physically able to slow and lift – at least for a few strides – but he refused to sustain the movement and then objected. The rearing didn't seem malicious, and each time Kluedo was then willing to go forwards again. He just seemed to be giving a clear message that he found the new activity difficult, and perhaps uncomfortably demanding.

It was time for us to think outside the box. If the longer-term goal of Kluedo's training was to help him progress to more advanced work, he would need to build strength and confidence in carrying himself energetically more 'in place' and less forwards. Yet asking him directly for this produced a firm: 'No – can't'. I came up with the idea of using spirals to get Kluedo engaging and stepping under (only putting pressure on one hind leg instead of two, since in spirals it's the inside hind that has to engage more), and Kluedo was quite prepared to do this without protest. And Sean came up with the idea of using slow, energetic shoulder-in through and out of the corners of the school to achieve the same effect – which Kluedo was also able to achieve without difficulty and without protest.

Switching to these movements respected Kluedo's physical difficulty, and his apparent alarm, at being asked for something entirely new. Yet each required him to engage and carry himself more that he had previously had to. By chunking down creatively, we were able to respect Kluedo's response without labelling him 'difficult' or 'uncooperative,' and yet substitute exercises which still related to Sean's longer-term goal. By the end of the session, Kluedo was calmly and effortlessly progressing in the direction Sean wanted: the slow, engaged, cadenced trot was, in the event, too big a chunk for Kluedo to manage on this occasion either physically or mentally. He simply needed another stage in between.

10

Traps and States

WHEN WE'RE WORKING alone we're in a kind of bubble, in which our own thoughts and feelings determine what's going on. They're as much the 'reality' we experience as the 'reality' of the outside world, because they determine to a large extent how we interpret the information that's coming to us from outside. In this chapter I want to show you some ways to manage some of the common pitfalls of solo schooling. I've called them **traps** and **states**. And I want to introduce a concept that can transform your day-to-day riding and help take it forward. It's the concept of PLAY and, paradoxically, what we know about how people learn demonstrates that play is definitely the most rapid, effective – and joyous – way.

Traps

In talking with solo schoolers and with expert trainers, I kept hearing again and again about the same problems. I've called them traps because they actually involve not a single event but a process, in which something that happens externally, or something you think, sets off an entire process that ends up with you feeling negative and becoming less effective. You've been *trapped* into a *state* in which you've become less resourceful. And, as the aim of this book is to get you – and keep you – resourceful, we need to look at what can interfere with this condition, and see how you can return to being resourceful again if it does.

The NLP idea of the logical levels, which we looked at earlier, helps us to sort out where these difficulties are occurring.

Problems of Capability

If you don't have the knowledge or the skill to do something, you can take action: read a book; have a lesson; borrow a schoolmaster so that you can get the feel of an advanced movement that's new to you. Lack of capability isn't, in itself, a problem – what makes it become a trap is how you respond to it.

When I first started to learn dressage, I took our schoolmaster, Tristan, to an unaffiliated Riding Club show. I'd already done one dressage test on a friend's horse, and was quite pleased to get some sevens as well as some fives (actually, I had my test sheet framed to mark the achievement). However, Tristan is part Thoroughbred, and easily gets worked up, and competing with him was a much more tense affair. In fact, we were both so anxious that it affected our communication. When I asked for canter, hanging on desperately in front because I was (probably rightly) afraid that Tristan would bomb off if I didn't, what he produced felt rather 'lumpy'. It was only when I looked at the test sheet that I understood: he'd been so confused and tight that he'd produced a series of flying changes each time we cantered. The judge commented pretty coolly on the tension and the hanging on in front. I felt so stupid and inadequate that I didn't compete again for more than two years. There was a practical problem – Tristan and I weren't communicating effectively. But, much worse, was my feeling of inadequacy and the state of despair it got me into.

This was a temporary capability issue. Learning more and becoming more skilful and confident made me more effective, and owning my dislike of competition made me more content to be how I am. But what about when you realize that you, or your horse, are never going to have the ability to do what you want? Perhaps you're too old, or not athletic enough. Perhaps he's the same. That's the 'away from'. Sometimes the trap here is that your assessment of the situation is more limited (and limiting) than it need be. Some dressage judges will tend to mark down cobs or ponies because they 'don't have the paces'. Others, however, will recognize that a rhythmical, attentive pony, accurately ridden, is in fact producing good dressage. I've also seen wonderfully effective communication and fluent tests produced by elderly, arthritic riders, riders with physical handicaps, and horses whose build made certain kinds of movement difficult or impossible.

If you are (or your horse is) limited in any of these ways, the trick is to avoid making negative assumptions, and to go for the most you can achieve, because that way you're pushing your boundaries, not confining yourself.

By this, I don't mean just bash on regardless. If you have a heavy cob who's built on the forehand, or an ex-racehorse whose movement is fast and flat, lengthened strides are going to present a problem. Don't just come round the corner and belt off across the diagonal. Practise at home, setting your partner up before the corner with a half-halt and some extra inside leg to improve his balance and increase his engagement – and then ask for just a few lengthened strides, so that he has every chance of showing a difference and keeping his balance. And return to the working gait as soon as he has done so, so that you show his accomplishment rather than allowing him to spoil it all by ploughing onto his forehand as he loses balance again.

If, on reflection, you accept that you and your partner have really reached your limits, be honest with yourself – but without judging yourself harshly. The problem is not the limitation itself, but whether you give yourself a bad time over it, thus getting yourself into an unresourceful state. Advanced riders can get just as worked up about problems with changes, or piaffe, as novices do about problems at lower levels. The trick is to be dispassionate. Assess the situation from third position, as a concerned observer – and then ask 'what else can we do?' Remember that the Dreamer can help you find new possibilities and new directions, and that the true Critic looks for good points as well as spotting limitations. There will always be something you can not only do, but can do well.

Behavioural Traps

I think there are three main behavioural traps for solo schoolers:

1. Playing safe.

2. Not being 'in the moment'.

3. Getting stuck in repetition.

Playing safe

Playing safe is self-protective – that's its great benefit. But we don't learn or accomplish anything new when we're in our safety zone. The key is to decide when it's useful to play safe and when it isn't. If you're tired, or unwell, or feeling vulnerable for other reasons, play safe: it will increase your chances of achieving what you want, of having a good time, and of feeling pleased with what you've done. If your horse is feeling tired, or anxious, play safe: these are not good conditions for asking him to try something new. Make it a part of your self-coaching to assess what you're both up for today, and what you're not, and respect that it's right and proper to do so. That's a coach's job, and it's just as much your job when you're coaching yourself.

When you do decide that it's time to stretch your limits, play safe in another way. Try for just a little of what you want; aim for an approximation to it, not for being perfect. Play with the new skill or the new challenge. Toe dip. Make it easy for yourself and your horse to try it out – and reward yourselves, even if you know there's still a long way to go. This is another place for honesty, both in recognizing that you haven't got there yet and also in accepting that you have begun the journey.

Not being 'in the moment'

Riding is an in-time activity, meaning that you have to take information and respond to it moment by moment. In Chapter 4: Triangulation, I showed how we can enhance our in-the-moment experience by referring to the past and glancing ahead to the future. But, rather like looking in your rear-view mirror, or monitoring what's happening three cars ahead when you're driving, you need most of your attention in the here-and-now. As a teenager, my mother used to be late for breakfast – and for school – because she had been so busy imagining herself getting up and ready that she hadn't actually moved out of bed! And I've known riders so involved in what they will be doing three movements ahead in their test, or six weeks away when they've cracked some particular problem, that they missed doing what was needed right now. Fast reverse, fast forward by all means, so long as you relocate in the moment again. As the case-study of Marisian shows, the best time for review and planning is when you're not actually riding. That's why riders have so often found it helpful to work in that way with me, even on the phone: this form of coaching, and self-coaching, both have valuable, but different, parts to play in working towards your goals.

Repetition

If at first you don't succeed, try, try, try again. NLP has a counter-argument to this old adage: *If you always do what you've always done, you'll always get what you've always got.*

When does practice become a trap, and how do you know? I'd say, when practice isn't making any difference. When you're beginning to feel bored, frustrated or angry. When your horse is losing concentration or getting stroppy. And, at the other end of the scale, when you've done something as well as you both possibly could. Don't go on.

- If things aren't improving, it's time for a new approach, a new strategy or just a break. It may be time for a rethink away from the saddle.

- Boredom, frustration and anger are all strong feelings, so they will inevitably contaminate your ability to converse clearly and calmly with your horse. Stop. Do something different, which you know you can both easily accomplish. These kinds of feelings tell my friend Marisian that it's time she simply got off. There is no merit in slogging on – and nothing is gained by it. Get out of the situation and, in your own time, find a way to change it.

- When you've jumped that difficult spread, or done your first excellent shoulder-in, or those few steps of passage, stop right there. New achievements are often fragile, and the two of you may not yet be able to do it again. If you fail, your achievement will feel tarnished and insubstantial. Worst of all, you may even be tempted to try again – and perhaps 'fail' again. You will have converted your wonderful success into a miserable disappointment. Leave well alone. Pat your horse, cherish yourself. Let the good feeling, and the reward, work their reinforcing magic. Wait for another day.

Problems of Belief

In my experience there are three kinds of belief issues that can really obstruct you from enjoying and developing your riding. These are:

1. Reliance on the expertise of others (*implied belief: 'They are better/know more*).

2. A sense of your own limitations (*implied belief: 'I'm not good enough'*).

3. Knowing that something isn't perfect (*implied belief: 'I'll never be good enough'*).

Reliance on others

Relying on others to judge your performance can make you doubt your own judgement, and end up with you becoming dependent. When I asked one rider I was helping what she wanted to achieve from our session together, she said '*I don't know. No one has asked me that question before'*. What she was used to was riding in front of her trainer and being told: told how her horse was going, told what he needed to do better, and told how to achieve it. She had a competent teacher, who almost certainly wouldn't have wanted to make her dependent – but that was the result produced by the way they worked together. This rider found it quite hard to think for herself, and even though she was knowledgeable enough to assess what her horse was doing, she still waited for me to suggest what strategies she might use, rather than tapping into her own knowledge for ideas. In fact, she told me that she had got so used to being directed in her riding that she no longer felt confident in schooling on her own. She had become teacher-dependent.

If you are in a similar position, consider retraining yourself gradually. Make sure that you have some solo sessions between your regular lessons, and take one, or at the most two, ideas from your last instructed lesson as pegs to hang your own schooling upon. This will give you something to work with – but it will be *you* working with it. Let yourself pause every few minutes to review what's been going on; take a third-position view of yourself and your horse and comment on what you've noticed. Give yourself homework – and use time away from the saddle to think through what's happened and to plan for next time. Sandwich your self-coaching in between sessions where you are being taught by someone else. Perhaps add to your skills by helping a friend from the ground: observing her and coaching her will increase your confidence and give you more ideas for helping yourself.

A sense of your own limitations

It's easy to move from knowing your limitations to being self-critical. It's easy to get into conversations with yourself where you pick on your repeated faults – *'There goes my wobbly left hand again'; 'I never remember to keep my outside leg back in canter'; 'I know about half-halts, so why do I never use them?'* Internal dialogue like this is a great way of making yourself feel even more inadequate. Recognizing a pattern can give you really helpful information; but once you start adding words like 'ever', 'never' and 'always' – even in the privacy of your own thoughts – you make yourself feel helpless and condemned to stay like that. These words imply that a pattern has always been there and will always remain there. So the pattern you've noticed is no longer neutral information: it's now a trap. And it gets you into the state that goes with being trapped.

Coaching doesn't make judgements like this. It certainly does involve noticing patterns, and giving people feedback on them. But, because it's done in a spirit of curiosity, it feels more like someone saying *'Hey, isn't it interesting how that outside leg of yours slides forward once you've got the canter going. I wonder what that's about. I wonder what would need to happen for it to stay back.'* And that kind of feedback prompts search, produces more information and gets you searching for solutions. The implied belief here is that with more information and experimentation, things are fixable.

When I started coaching riders, I wondered how to avoid telling them that they were doing something 'wrong'. It seemed over-elaborate, and almost dishonest, to avoid telling them how it was. Then I realized that a coach doesn't avoid telling someone how it is. Coaches quite often give feedback. But because a coach is on your side, and you have established a cooperative way of working together to achieve goals that you've chosen, feedback remains just that. It's extra information. So nowadays I won't disguise or try to soften my feedback – for example, by saying 'Tell me what's going on in the small of your back'. I might, instead, say something like 'I notice your back tends to hollow when you make a downward transition. Tell me how that feels. What's going on there? What happens if you round it instead?' The questions I'm asking are genuine, because I don't know the answers. But the rider does – when the question prompts them to search.

The sequence of *observation > feedback > search > further experimentation > evaluation > observation, etc.* is a powerful tool for learning. The implied belief is that we're all capable of learning and improving. We have what it takes.

This is a good pattern to remember when you're coaching yourself, because when you're interacting with yourself you can have just the same good, or bad, effects that an external trainer can. Believing that you have what it takes to go down the *observation > feedback > search > further experimentation > evaluation > observation* route is a great enabler. Life has already taught you what's involved in any of these areas, and regularly using your skills in self-coaching will certainly help you to improve them even further.

Knowing that something isn't perfect

If you watch great performers in any discipline, you are likely to know that what you do doesn't quite match up. This can be infuriating, if it presses your *'if only'* button, or dispiriting if it presses your *'I'll never be able to'* button. And in this frame of mind, however good you are, *better* is always just out of reach. However well you do it, whatever it is, it's not perfect – and it never will be.

Perfectionism is a double-edged tool. Striving for the best can have the effect of inspiring you – but endlessly comparing yourself with the unattainable can turn you off and send you into the depths of gloom.

I remember watching a really able rider having a lesson on her talented horse with Charles de Kunffy. Overall, the horse was going well, and de Kunffy commented on how much he had improved since the previous lesson six months earlier. Then he drew the rider's attention to one thing that needed improving – and I saw her face and posture change, reflecting disappointment and irritation. When I talked with her afterwards, she said how upset she felt.

'But he said how well the horse was going and how much he's improved,' I said.

'That's not what I heard,' she replied.

Because this particular rider is a perfectionist, she filters the feedback she gets so that she takes in what she has to do to improve – but that, of course, reinforces her belief that she isn't perfect. She finds it almost impossible to give equal weight to praise when it comes at the same time as suggestions for improvement.

Since perfection can never be attainable, it can never be a well-formed outcome. If you tend to be a perfectionist, remind yourself that the idea of perfection is, at best, what de Kunffy calls 'How the Greats do it'. And even the great performers aren't perfect – how can any two living beings be perfect? The breathtaking skills of some riders, and the brilliant performances which they build with their horses, don't need to be standards we strive to match. Rather, we can use them as compass bearings to help us go in the right direction. Riding is a journey which begins every time you mount up. Whether yesterday's ride was wonderful or awful, or somewhere in between, today is a new start – if you treat it like one.

If you are aiming to liberate yourself from the tramline of striving for perfection, you may need to retrain yourself gradually. Be sure, when you evaluate how a session has gone, to look for things that went well, for experiments that seemed promising – and to identify just how you achieved them. Write these points down, if it helps. I'd suggest you write on every other line, leaving space for editing later. Then read over what you've written, and put a line through judgemental words like 'good', 'bad', 'well' and 'successful'. These shorthand labels all plug you back into perfectionism and the success/failure way of thinking. Next, use your empty lines to fill in the hard evidence that made you reach those judgements. Finally, make a list of 'things I can be pleased with – and my skills in achieving them'. Mark it out in some way – perhaps with a highlighter. When next you are feeling low about your riding, look at your notes again, and your eye will automatically be drawn to these encouraging points. These are the riches you already have – and they are essential to your progress on many levels. Treasure them and make the most of them.

There is one other problem with perfectionism. Aiming for perfection can put you into a 'trying' state – and this usually disables you because, as Timothy Gallwey discovered, it's one of the greatest sources of interference. Trying is not the same as involvement or commitment. It's about effort and a lack of experimentation. Trying, in fact, is the opposite of play – and I'm asking you to take the coaching view that play is the way forward, as I'll explain more fully later in this chapter.

States

The traps I've been describing all get you into unresourceful mind-body states. There's a great range of states that can interfere with riding: stiffening up because of 'trying' or being self-critical, freezing or becoming frantic through fear, becoming despondent and lethargic… Take your pick. And every one of these will interfere with the conversation you're trying to have with your horse. States such as these create a kind of interfering 'white noise', that blocks and distorts the messages passing between the two of you. Happy states don't seem to have the same effect, because they so often mean you are relaxed. And a state of mental relaxation often gets transmitted as an ease and fluency at a physical level, so that smaller signals are clearer and more effective: transmission and reception – both ways – become easier and more effective.

Breaking State

Perhaps the best way to describe the kind of state you want is one of relaxed absorption. Gallwey calls it 'focus'. We could also use the kinesthetic word 'centred', or the auditory phrase 'in tune'.

But what if the state you're in currently isn't at all like this? Remember that states have both mental and physical elements. If you're finding it hard to snap out of a black mood, or energize yourself, the easiest thing you can do is to **break state** – and the easiest way to do this is to change your physiology. If you're feeling sluggish, changing position or posture is a start. You may be amazed at how much difference there is between slumping and sitting upright, between standing and walking, between walking and running, between a dismal attempt at collected trot and a brisk extended canter along the long side… By changing any one element, you change the overall pattern: you've changed state. And as you change the physiology, it makes it hard to maintain the emotion or the thought pattern that went with it. You've broken the mould.

You can also use your physiology as leverage to help your horse change his state. You can 'mismatch' – for example, by deliberately rising to the trot in a slower rhythm than your horse. Since he will find this strange, he will tend to alter his own rhythm to match yours. Even more dramatic is insisting on rising to a non-existent trot when you don't want your horse to canter: again, the mismatch is likely to cause him to break his excited state and get him matching and listening to you again. Or you can use sound. I tend to sing to our horses when they get excited out hacking, or on the lunge, first matching the fast rhythm of their movement and then slowing down the tempo until they follow my lead.

Once you've broken the state you don't want, you are in a position to create the one you do want. You can reinforce it by maintaining or adopting the physiology that goes with it, or by calling up your memories of how you feel when you are in that state. As you tap into those memories, you give yourself the best chance of recreating the feelings, thoughts and behaviour that go along with them. Working with Nikki one day, I asked her to tell me how she thought Lolly was going. She said that he felt 'Mellow but not forward, not like when he's gung-ho sometimes'. I asked her to remember how he felt when he was forward and gung-ho – and, even though he was only walking in warm-up, Lolly's energy and the length and purpose of his stride all increased. Later on the same day, when she was riding her own horse, Merlin, I asked her to remember 'the best walk he's ever given you' – and then 'the best trot'. Simply going into her own stored experience through active internal search was enough to change Nikki's state – and her horse's behaviour – quite profoundly. You might like to experiment with this too.

The State of Play

As adult learners, tending to struggle with all sorts of baggage, we can in fact learn a great deal from the way that all children learn naturally – and we have our own first-hand memory store of how that was. And the key to this natural learning is a state that I'd like you to explore as a way of making your riding both more enjoyable and more effective. It's the state of PLAY.

Children are the best players and the best learners – and they get really involved in their play. The play of very young children is full of experiments and discoveries, and that's the kind of play we need to recapture. How would it be to feel like that about your riding?

How can you cultivate this – and how can you return to it when something has got you into a less resourceful state? Let's use the word PLAY itself as a key.

P stands for **Permission** and for **Pleasure**.

L stands for **Learning**.

A stands for **Action**.

Y stands for a **Yes** attitude.

Permission

This is the first step. You may have to work quite hard at allowing yourself to stop trying so hard! You may have to work at changing long-standing beliefs that, because you are committed to your riding, you have to 'take it seriously'. Oscar Wilde said that anything worth doing is worth doing badly. If you only allow yourself to do something that you can be sure of doing well, you'll never learn anything new. You need to give yourself permission to have a go, to be less than perfect, to experiment and to discard some of your experiments while pursuing others.

Pleasure

Pleasure is another great key to learning. When you enjoy something, it's so much easier to learn, and to remember what you've learnt. And since, in riding, you are in a mutual teaching-learning relationship with another creature, you need to ensure that he takes pleasure in it all, too. Pleasure comes from noticing and enjoying *what is*, not focusing on what isn't, or can't be. It comes from small things. It comes from variety. It comes from the unexpected. You can ensure that your riding is varied, and that you and your horse don't get bored. We've taken to mixing our schooling sessions sometimes with a little jumping, which the horses enjoy. Sometimes we jump to help them stretch over the back and warm up, sometimes to relax them and let them down after working precisely and in a more collected outline. On other occasions we have a short hack either before or after schooling. Or we might loose school them so that they can use themselves freely. Within a ridden session, we try to vary the work so that repetition doesn't lead to boredom or physical strain. The aim is to make every ride enjoyable, for both partners.

Learning

Play is a great state for learning, because when you're playing, you're really paying attention to your experience. You're likely to be 'in the moment' (in-time), and using each of your senses. You're involved. This means that you're in the right state for observation, experimentation and discovery. Much of your playful learning will be occurring effortlessly at an unconscious level – your conscious mind may only 'catch up' with what you've learnt later. You'll usually get more out of twenty minutes of playful riding than forty minutes of dogged working at it. And when it stops being playful, it's a signal that something needs to change.

Action

Action can be physical or mental, or both, but without action you won't be in a fully engaged and resourceful state. You might be switched off, or just passive, but action is what engages you – just like your horse. Unless he has a desire to go forward, he can't be engaged. It's the engagement of his hind legs that gives you power and can develop into self-carriage as he learns to lift and carry rather than just push himself along. It's engagement through his back and neck

Action – Marisian and Prudie.

muscles that saves wear and tear on his joints and allows him to round up and drape himself naturally and effortlessly onto the bit. And it's your mental and physical actions that get you engaged too.

When I asked the case-study riders what was different about being coached, as compared to being taught, they all said that coaching got them more active in their minds. Sometimes this felt like hard work, but it also got them more involved. One said that, whereas a session of instruction, based on doing what the trainer asked, could be useful and satisfying, coaching involved more thinking and discussion, and seemed to result in the horses going better and winning more. So what made this happen? In my experience of coaching people on a wide range of life and business issues, it's being engaged in the processes of discovery, experimentation and purposeful change that makes all the difference. Coaching is a process which insists on you being active, so it draws out your energy and helps you to focus it on your needs and your goals.

'Yes' attitude

When we play, we're wanting to do what we're doing: we're saying 'yes' to our experience and the opportunities it gives us. 'Yes' produces great states: excitement, commitment, inventiveness and delight. While a 'yes' sense can be triggered accidentally by what's happening, it can also be set up deliberately – and this is the point I want to make here. You can cultivate a 'yes' attitude in yourself and in your horse. Here are some ways to do it:

- Make sure that you always begin with things you can already do easily, and finish your riding session either with something similar or at a moment of accomplishment, so that you encourage yourselves and reward yourselves with that 'yes' feeling.

- Use the word 'yes!' to mark achievements. Said out loud, it becomes a reinforcement for both you and your horse. Said silently inside your head, it has the same effect for you and will almost certainly be transmitted to your horse through your body language. (This means that you can say it, and benefit from its effects, even in the middle of a silent dressage competition!)

- Chunk your larger goals down into smaller, achievable steps to increase the probability of success – and of being able to say 'yes' to them.

- Remember that a 'yes' approach can be cultivated in everything you do with your horse. Try to set up everything you ask of him in the stable as well as in

a.   b.

the school so that it's easy for him to say 'yes' to you. This reinforces a habit of cooperation between you, and builds confidence and trust for times when you have to ask him to do something he finds alarming or difficult. It also means you avoid some conflicts that may be unnecessary.

Engagement and reward at the end of a good session.
(a) Sean and Georgie;
(b) Nicky and Lucinda.

What's the first thing you can do to bring PLAY into your riding?
How can you make it a regular part of your riding life?

In understanding the traps that may await you as a rider, and learning how you can break and create the states you are in, you have acquired some very important tools for shaping the way you do your solo schooling. In the chapters that follow, I'm going to explore two key features of the coaching approach that can help you make your schooling more purposeful and effective. The first is the use of questions, and the second is the way in which you structure your schooling sessions. Together, these provide the way in which you can use all the other tools to best effect, because they provide the real 'edge' of your self-coaching.

Playtime –
Wendy and Nikki G

As I showed in the previous chapter, play, with its attendant state of attentive, pressure-free curiosity, is a productive and delightful state in which to ride. A while ago, Nikki and I had one of our regular coaching exchanges, in which first she coached me on Lolly, then immediately afterwards I coached her on Beamish. What happened between us really illustrates the kind of processes I've been writing about.

As I warmed up Lolly and myself, Nikki asked me what I wanted to work on. I told her how I had recently been experimenting with minimal aiding, using my weight for steering and the timing of my out-breath to cue Lolly for downward transitions – as, for example, in simple changes. I felt that this had been really useful in making our communication more subtle and stylish. Nikki pointed out that using an out-breath like this was a form of half-halt, and this got us thinking about other ways of making half-halts.

Riders often find half-halts mysterious – and even writers on horsemanship have different ways of describing what's involved. As Nikki and I shared the various ways we knew of giving a half-halt, we realized that we were talking about a variety of signals which were rather like the many different intonations you can use to say the word 'no'. (Practise for a moment and you'll realize how huge a variety you can produce.)

Here are some ways we thought of:

• Sitting more upright (rider rebalances > horse rebalances).

• Sitting deeper (done correctly, this encourages the horse to step more under and come 'through' the back).

• Flattening the shoulder-blades (stabilizes the elbows and brings them closer to the rider's sides, firming the frame into which the horse is working and thus asking him to collect).

• Taking a big breath and letting it out (relaxes the rider's diaphragm and deepens the seat; probably also acts as an auditory 'pause' signal to the horse).

• Giving a small upward tweak to the reins without bringing the hand back at all (signals to horse to take weight off forehand and come up in front, without making him hollow or disengage).

You may be able to think of others.

Speculating like this got us wanting to experiment, so Nikki asked me to play with just my breathing – speeding it up and slowing it down. When I started cantering around her in a circle, altering my breathing at the same time, Nikki immediately noticed that Lolly's expression became very attentive and he turned his ears sideways in order to listen better. Then he began to respond to the breathing signals – faster, shallower breaths from me led to more energy and longer strides from him; slower, deeper breaths cued him to shorten his stride and become more collected. This was exciting stuff!

Sean half-halting Kluedo by breathing out during a tense moment at the Winter Finals.

When it was time for me to coach Nikki, we agreed that we would stay well within Beamish's comfort zone, as he hadn't worked for three days because of a cut on his leg. However, we could easily continue to explore the effects of breathing. In Nikki's case, this served another purpose, because she has always tended to collapse at her waist.

As I watched her I remembered a martial arts exercise which is used to help lower the centre of gravity, thus making the person more securely grounded and less vulnerable to being pushed off balance. I wondered whether Nikki (perhaps other riders, too) – might be collapsing in the waist in an instinctive attempt to bring her centre of gravity closer to that of the horse. If so, lowering it through a mental rather than a physical process should allow her to remain more upright. And this was what we found. Nikki immediately sat up taller – making more space for her lungs and diaphragm so that it was easier for her to control how and when she breathed, and easier to ride Beamish 'uphill'.

So we discovered that several factors might be at work in this situation. One seemed to be related to where Nikki had her centre of gravity. Another was breathing. On this occasion Nikki was in a relaxed and experimental state, but she has often 'tried' too hard – and often when riders are trying something new, or 'trying hard' to get something right, they simply 'forget' to breathe. Not only does this deprive them of a subtle range of signals, but it may actually give their horse just the signals they don't want to give: rapid, shallow, puffing breath can speed the horse up or confuse him, because for him it's part of the body-profiling he will associate with excite/flight states in himself and other horses.

What we found as Nikki played with brief periods of slow trot was that her own repositioning gave her more space to breathe, and this in turn helped Beamish to engage more and lighten his forehand. She was able to make trot to walk transitions, as I had, just on the out-breath, and Beamish also became more energetic and lengthened his stride in response to a faster breathing pattern. When, after about twenty minutes, he produced the lightest, most 'uphill' and cadenced trot Nikki had ever received from him, we decided to stop: we'd all achieved more than we could have hoped for. Nikki and I had found our shared and playful exploration stimulating and fun, and from Lolly's attentive, curious expression and Beamish's unusually serene demeanour, we were pretty sure that they had, too.

PART 4

Coaching in Action

11

Coaching Yourself with Questions

THE KEY TO COACHING is curiosity, and it's questions that open up curiosity. A statement tells you something: it defines your range of response, and as a listener, your response is to react with a 'yes', 'no', or 'maybe'. A question sets you off on an internal search of some kind: you are looking for an answer. And the answer, particularly to an 'open' question (one that asks for more than just a 'yes' or 'no' response) will very often be bigger than the question. This is why people who have received coaching often comment that they have felt more involved, and have contributed more to the results they got. Their coach's questions have got them finding their own answers. In this chapter I'm going to look at how you can use questions to coach and involve yourself – and your horse.

Leading Questions

There's an important point to make here, and that is that the questions have to be genuine. As a coach, you're faking if you ask a question to which you already know the answer. If you can see that someone's horse is falling sideways in halt because the rider's weight is all to one side, it's not really coaching to ask *'Why did your horse fall sideways in the halt?'* You're actually just inviting the rider to try to guess the 'right' answer, confirming a dependence on you rather than adding to the rider's own resourcefulness. However, if you ask questions like *'What did you notice just then?'*, or *'What messages do you think he was getting as you came into the halt?'*, or *'How do you think you could help him stay more in balance as he halts?'*, you are sending the rider off on a search which can access more information, promote different methods of evaluation and stimulate experimentation. All of these processes will get the rider more involved.

The same is true if you are coaching yourself. *'Why on earth did I do that?'* is likely to make you feel cross with yourself and reinforce your sense of incompetence, or even failure. *'What was going on there?'*, however, gets you thinking.

So a coaching question is one that sends you off in search of the unknown, and its potential is that it helps you discover information that gives you more to work with. Coaching questions can have a number of possible functions:

• They can get you sorting through information you already have – *What made that halt so much crisper than the last one?*

• They can help you seek for information you had unconsciously but weren't aware of at a conscious level – *My horse tends to fall to the right in halt. Is there a difference between the way I put my legs on? Is my weight unbalanced to the right?*

• They can help you to focus on the specifics that are really the key to what's happening or not happening – for example, those details that NLP calls 'the difference that makes a difference' – *My horse sticks his head up when I ask for halt. Am I bringing my hands back? Or sitting too heavily? Or do I need more half-halts to prepare him first?*

• They can get you to specify exactly what evidence will tell you you've achieved something, thus helping you to gather relevant feedback and benchmark your progress – *What exactly will tell me, and the judge, that he's 'engaged into the halt'?*

Questions can achieve these results, but they have another important effect, too. They take the pressure off you – because the information they elicit about whatever is happening (or has happened) becomes something you can work with. The details of a 'problem' can thus often be transformed into a 'prescription' for improvement.

Search is one important result of curiosity and questioning and, as these examples show, it leads on to another valuable outcome. Searching brings up the evidence – external or internal – that tells you about what's going on, helps you to be specific about how exactly it's happening (or not happening!) and *takes you forward*. In coaching terms, information is interesting in itself, but the test of its value is whether it helps you progress towards your goals.

Search > Information > Forwarding the Action.

This is a useful formula to remember alongside Gallwey's *Performance = Potential – Interference,* described in Chapter 1.

It follows from this that you'll get further by asking yourself certain kinds of questions rather than others. As I said earlier in the book, '*why*' is the least useful way of beginning a question, because it gets you looking for reasons (and maybe justifications). It gets you reconstructing – often hypothetically – after the event.

'*Who*', '*how*', '*what*', '*where*' and '*when*' are much more useful starters, because they get you looking for specifics. And, where any skill is involved, probably the most useful question of all is '*how?*'

How?

'*How?*' leads you into what NLP calls modelling – which simply means taking what someone else does as a model for yourself, and learning to do what they do by finding out exactly how they do it. The simplest form of modelling is probably a recipe – but the more complex a skill gets the more it involves thinking, attitudes, beliefs and mind-body communication. If you're modelling achievement, or high degrees of physical skill, or great communication (all of which characterize good riding), then you need to model your exemplar at many levels. Modelling yourself is also very useful, because it helps you find out just how you do the things you do well, and just how you do the things you do less well. One of the great Sixties pop songs said it brilliantly:

How do you do what you do to me? I wish I knew.
If I knew how you do it to me, I would do it to you.

What?

'*How?*', then, is one of the great coaching questions. Here are some of the others, based upon '*what?*' Some of them have already been explored in the book, so I'll just remind you of them here.

What do I want?

What do I really, really want?

What stops me (doing x)?

What would happen if I did (do) x?

Other key questions are:

What specifically tells me (or will tell me)...?

This is the question that sends you off searching for the information you need in relation to a particular problem or aim.

What next?

This is the question that leads you into chunking down, and making your action-plan a do-able reality – do-able because it only asks you to think about a small step; reality because it makes you decide on a way forward.

And what else?

This is the question that gets you chunking laterally, thinking creatively, generating even more options. Asking this question is a great habit to get into, because it increases your tool-kit for influencing any situation. What else will achieve this effect? What else could you do in this situation? What else might be the cause? What else might result...? What else was going on, at this or other levels...?

Questioning Your Horse

Questioning yourself may seem relatively straightforward, once you think about it. But how can you question your horse? The answer is actually very simple: *whatever your horse does is his answer to the question he thought you asked him.*

NLP is the science of great communication, and one of the key observations made by the early developers of NLP was that people responded to what *they thought* a communication meant, rather than to what the communicator intended. This seems obvious – except that, when we're trying to tell someone something, we're often puzzled, frustrated or annoyed when they respond as if we'd actually said something different. That's because, in their understanding, we did. This is another of those issues where it's really useful to step outside the situation, take third position, and remind yourself that there's no right and wrong involved. Most people, and most horses, don't wilfully set out to misunderstand what you say to them. So what else is going on? And, if you want them to understand what you really do mean, how else are you going to try to make it clear to them?

If your horse doesn't do as you want, what can his behaviour tell you about what he thought you meant – or perhaps, what else he was attending to at the time? How else can you explain it to him?

Here are some of the questions you might ask of your horse in your solo schooling sessions together:

What's the clearest signal I can give you to...?

What's the smallest signal I can find that you will understand?

What range of signals do you understand?

What happens when I ask you this?

How do you let me know when you find something difficult? Too difficult?

Confusing/easy? Fun/alarming? Safe/dangerous?

Horses are actually very expressive – even facially – once we really pay attention to the exact ways we interact with each other. You will certainly find plenty of information on each of these questions, and in seeking and registering it you'll be refining the ways that you and your horse communicate and making them much subtler and more effective. You will be asking questions of your horse – and really listening to his answers. Good questioning, and attentive, thoughtful listening – to yourself and to your horse – will make your solo schooling more fascinating, more productive, and much more fun.

Questioning is a great way to guide your schooling and ensure its relevance and purpose. But even good questions need to be asked in the right way and at the right time. In the next chapter I'm going to show you how you can shape each and every solo schooling session so that it makes a purposeful and satisfying whole.

12

Structuring the Work Session

WHEN YOU RIDE ON YOUR own regularly, it can be easy to fill the time without having a defined shape to the session. One version of this is just getting on and pottering about. You may perhaps do a bit of this and a bit of that – a kind of smorgasbord of the movements you and your horse have in your repertoire; or you may warm up in a kind of mutual daze and never get much beyond that. And if you are riding first thing, before going to work, or in the evening after you have already used up much of your energy at work or home, it's really understandable.

We could think of this as riding **without focus**. At the other extreme, you might be so intent on practising a movement, or rehearsing a test, that this fills your mind and uses up most of the time. This is riding with **narrow focus**. If you are riding to a tight time schedule, or if you're a professional with a number of horses to ride, you may quite unconsciously find yourself shortening warm-up and tuning-in time because of the sense of urgency to get to the heart of the training you have planned. This can be **over-focus**.

For the solo schooler, the result of falling into each of these temptations is often a sense of disappointment or even failure. Where lack of focus leaves us wondering what on earth we did, narrow focus can produce a 'trying' state with its attendant tensions and success/failure frame, and over-focus may mean that horse and rider don't have time to tune in to each other properly and feel hassled and hurried in what they're doing. Usually, enjoyment has gone out of the window as well. In this chapter I want to suggest a simple pattern you can use to shape every session and ensure that it gives you and your horse something useful – one which on most occasions also loads your chances of having fun at the same time.

Once a coaching partnership has been established, most coaching sessions take about the same length of time as the core of a ridden schooling session – about thirty minutes. And it's amazing how much can be achieved in that time. When we work as coaches to ourselves, it's useful to bear in mind some important guidelines:

- Work with the agenda you have chosen – but keep alert for unexpected opportunities that may serve your larger goals.

- Stay focused on process, rather than getting distracted into too much detail of content: concern yourself not so much with *what* happened, but with *how* it happened, what contributed to it happening and what problems of action and reaction were at work.

- Be willing to experiment – and also willing to abandon experiments that don't seem to be working out.

- Respect your need to 'warm up' each time into the heart of your concerns, attend to what is observable, interesting and relevant so that you stand every chance of making progress, and make sure that you 'mark your learning' in some way. Agree with yourself what your next steps should be and, where appropriate, give yourself homework before the next session.

These points give us a quick summary of our objectives when we work alone. And each has its place in the simple three-stage format I'm about to suggest. I'm going to describe the stages briefly here, and then illustrate the process with an account of a session I had with Sean and Harry, one of his event horses, just before writing this.

Stage one: Warm-up
Tuning-in
Freeing and unblocking
Framing

Stage two: Workout
Exploring
Resourcing
Focusing and forwarding the action

Stage three: Cool-down

Unwinding

Celebrating

Marking the learning

Thinking forward

Let's explore these in a little more detail.

Stage One: Warm-up

Any athlete needs to warm up before training. Minds need focusing and bodies need to stretch and become limber. The blood needs to get moving, and the muscles need to become supple and responsive. Without warming-up, you can do damage, to yourself and your horse. This isn't a stage you should cut short, however tight your time-frame and however urgent the work you plan to do. If you have more than one horse to work, you may need to remind yourself that you need to start afresh each time. The temptation will come from feeling worked in yourself after the first one. *You* don't need to warm up any more – but your second, third or fourth horse does.

Tuning-in

It may help if you remind yourself that the ten or fifteen minutes you need to allow for work in walk, or in a long, loose frame, gives you a wonderful opportunity for tuning-in to your horse. How is he today? Alert or sluggish? Stiff or relaxed? Anxious and distracted, or calm and attentive? This is a time for you to match his mood and pace (see Chapter 6) to increase the rapport between you. Rapport is the base of attentiveness and trust on which you can build the play, experimentation and discovery that is to come in the heart of the session.

Freeing and Unblocking

Once you have both warmed up, you will be aware of, and can zero in on, anything that seems to be blocking fluency, either between the two of you, or in one or other of you. Asking for more energy and swing in the basic gaits will reveal any physical tightness or mental distraction and allow you to work out what's needed to unblock it. This is the time to work long and low, to ride big shapes, to change direction, to do exercises that aid suppleness, to alternate rising and sitting trot, light seat and deeper seat. It's the time to use your weight to check responsiveness, to play with signals of different strength for changes of speed and direction, to spiral in and out or leg-yield to remind both partners of the leg aids.

Framing

Monitoring in this way will begin to tell you what needs particular attention today – either in the sense of building on the opportunities your horse seems to be offering, or in the sense of helping with what you or he are finding difficult. It's a time to check your own state and ensure that you're framing the session in ways that are productive rather than limiting. Are you irritated? Are you feeling driven? Are you feeling blocked? If so, return to freeing and unblocking for a while longer, while you sort yourself out.(Nicky describes such a moment in her account of our work together, see page 202.)

Stage Two: Workout

This is the core of the session. Sometimes you don't realize what this is at the time – only afterwards. On other occasions, you know just what you're zooming in on, and why. The workout is a state of full attentiveness and engagement, involving you both, and it can feel marvellous even if it lasts only a few minutes. In fact, it doesn't need to last long, because it's about purposeful activity leading to learning, consolidation or achievement. In fact, knowing when to stop is one of the solo schooling arts to cultivate, as I've explained elsewhere (see p 162). We can so easily 'take the bloom off' good work by over-doing it and, in the process, lose the sense of excitement, discovery and achievement. Stopping at a peak moment leaves these great feelings intact, as a proper reward, and carries a good mood forward to the next time.

Exploring

When you work in a state of playful attentiveness with your horse, you will be exploring: exploring what it takes to give and receive a particular message, exploring variations on that message and their different results, noticing and reflecting on the feedback you give each other. This can be like a really good conversation, speculating together on something of interest to you both.

Resourcing

As you explore, you begin to be aware of what might be needed to help you with any difficulties you are having, or to take you further. Resources include external things like schooling patterns (for example, more shoulder-in to engage his inside hind, more work without stirrups to deepen your seat) and internal things like managing your state ('Forget riding after work, I'm always too tired and rushed' – so why not try getting up earlier and riding before work instead). They can also include capability issues, like recognizing that it's time to get more information about the aids for half-pass, or some help with getting your inside shoulder back on turns.

Focusing and Forwarding the Action

This phase may be very brief, because it involves those moments or minutes of intense focus which are the heart of playful learning. It's the time when you refine something enough to feel you've made a difference. In our coaching model, this is in strong contrast to a 'trying' state. Where 'trying' can communicate itself to your horse and may well deaden the spark essential to purpose and fluency, focus is about willing, even joyful, engagement at every level of mind and body. It's about how you are, as much as what you achieve. And forwarding the action is just that: taking things forward not only in what you do, but also in how you think, how you feel, how he understands, how you communicate with each other. Forwarding the action means getting movement anywhere in the mind-body systems – his, yours or shared – that takes you in the direction you want to go. Sometimes it's a little; sometimes it's a lot. And you always know it when you've got it.

Stage Three: Cool-down

Celebrating

As soon as you have that 'yes' feeling, make sure that you celebrate it. Stroke your horse quietly. Avoid those great slaps on the neck, however joyful you feel. Celebration isn't boisterous – boisterous is the happy equivalent of swearing, and just about as useless for aiding true communication. You want your horse to know he's done well, and to feel good about it. If he's been working in a shortened frame, loosen the rein and let him stretch. Walk quietly. Or do something he really enjoys – a loping canter down the long side; a couple of little jumps; a walk up the lane.

Unwinding

Muscles need time to cool down, so take a few minutes or so to get both of your breaths back, moving with freedom and relaxation so that you don't get chilled. Unwind mentally by allowing your focus to open up as well. Look around – notice the weather, the birds, what's going on around you.

Marking the Learning

While you're unwinding, ask yourself what you learnt today. Timothy Gallwey found that this was a great way of helping his clients to progress. By reflecting at the end of a session on what it had meant for them – what they'd noticed, and asking themselves what they would be taking away from it – they put the experience into their own form of coding, so that it was properly stored and therefore easily remembered and retrieved. If they didn't do this, the learning lacked clarity and sometimes even tended to slip away. It's rather like trying to remember the name of someone you're introduced to at a party. If you really pay attention to them and to their name as it's being said, and remind yourself of it a couple of times immediately afterwards, you will find it much easier to remember later on. If you don't, the name and face aren't going to be filed firmly into your own personal storage system, so they won't be there when you want them again.

Thinking Forward

Finally, as you put your horse back in the stable or the field and take yourself home, ask yourself what needs to come next. How can you test out the validity of what you discovered through your experimentation, take it on, or usefully extend its application? Allow yourself to speculate. Finish with a curiosity frame, which sets you up for continued explorations and inquiries at many levels.

Warm-up, workout and cool-down: these then, are three phases that, together, shape each session and help it become an enjoyable and productive experience for you and your horse. Like all guidelines, you'll find that these can have exceptions – but if you use them as a basis, you will be aware of anything you're skipping or shortening, and why. In one session I had with Lolly, he made it emphatically clear, as soon as I was in the saddle, that he wasn't interested in his usual gentle warm-up: he was fit, energetic and supple enough to skip his normal ten minutes of walk and start off in a sparky trot. Tuning-in meant accepting that this was how he felt – and letting him know that it was fine with me. We could go straight to loosening, having already 'agreed' a frame of energetic playfulness.

Having this overall structure in your mind means that it will become an automatic way of shaping your solo schooling. Sometimes you won't even be aware that you're coaching yourself through these phases – but you will be doing it all the same. And, as you do, you'll be putting together all that you've learnt about self-coaching into an elegant, effective and 'seamless' whole: solo schooling at its powerful and exciting best.

Structure in Action – Sean and Harry

Harry is an Intermediate event horse. Harry is sharp, which helps his cross-country but can cause him to lose concentration. He does not enjoy his dressage, and Sean has to coax him along. Under pressure, Harry will rear. 'We've come to an arrangement', Sean said. This means, in practice, that Sean doesn't ask for too much and, in exchange, Harry makes some concessions towards gathering himself together, working in a more or less rounded outline and doing the required movements.

Harry is like many event horses in his response to dressage, and I thought that it would be particularly interesting to see how far we could get with a playful, experimental approach to flatwork.

Warm-up

Tuning-in; Freeing and unblocking; Framing

As we started, Sean told me that his strategy with Harry was to begin 'as though we're going for a hack'. Matching ('pacing') Harry meant riding on a loose rein

'Going for a hack'.
Sean and Harry at the
beginning of the
session.

at a relaxed way, almost mooching along. I noticed that Harry had very free action behind, stepping well under himself. On the other hand, the well-developed muscle on the underside of his neck told me that he spent most of his time *not* in a rounded outline – which, of course, then made it harder and more uncomfortable for him to do dressage at this more advanced level. When asked to halt or make downward transitions, Harry tended to over-round his neck and come behind the vertical rather than 'stepping through'. And because Sean was caught up in the same system, he tended to ask for these transitions by leaning back and coming behind the vertical himself, which in turn meant that Harry hollowed.

The warm-up work allowed me to recognize that the blocks which Harry and Sean experienced in their dressage work together related to Harry's lack of true engagement through from the hind legs to the bit. Sean had achieved a working arrangement which preserved their harmony together and, in fact, produced some very respectable dressage scores, yet without substantially impacting on Harry's basic difficulty.

Workout

Exploring; Resourcing; Focusing and forwarding the action

I wanted to help Sean to get Harry working more 'through' while, at the same time, respecting Harry's mental and physical reservations. Clearly, we needed some subtle strategies that would give Harry the experience of carrying himself in the way we wanted, and experiencing a greater connection through the back and neck without feeling driven or constricted into it. Having become fascinated by the effects of the rider's breathing on the horse, I wondered if Harry would respond to out-breaths as a 'passive' rather than an 'active' aid for the downward transitions, so this was what we played with next. Using his breathing rather than leaning back meant that Sean could maintain the light seat which Harry liked, maintaining his balance and existing centre of gravity while exerting an influence on the horse that was profound, yet not at all confrontational.

Structure in action – Sean using his breathing to influence the horse.

Harry was happier to carry himself in trot than in canter, and I wondered how we could offer him the opportunity of engaging more, but in a similarly 'easy' way in the latter gait. I remembered how Charles de Kunffy asks his riders to spin back their inside shoulder in time with the canter stride. This has the effect of enhancing the massaging effect of the inside seat bone on the horse's corresponding long back muscle, which in turn encourages the same-side hind leg to become more active in stepping under and lifting the horse instead of simply propelling him forwards. The rider can use the spin intermittently, for one or two strides, as an immediate rebalancing and collecting aid, or for longer periods to promote and maintain the engagement. Again, this is a non-confrontational yet very effective aid, and we found that Harry's balance and self-carriage improved without any apparent anxiety or resistance.

Spinning the inside shoulder back to rebalance and collect the horse.

Playing with these two strategies gave Sean some new resources for working with Harry at both physical and mental levels. Other strategies I suggested Sean might play with were sitting very upright and lengthening the front of his torso, so that he could more easily 'ride Harry uphill' in front of him, and using several half-halts prior to a downward transition to help Harry prepare and gather himself in readiness for the actual aid. These strategies

Sean sitting very upright and lengthening the front of his torso to ride Harry 'uphill'.

were all ones he could play with naturally in their future sessions together, and all would help set up the situation so that Harry would find himself working in greater balance, self-carriage and roundness without having to be formally 'asked'.

Cool-down

Unwinding; Celebrating; Marking the learning; Thinking forward

For the last part of the session Sean and Harry worked more freely in lengthening and shortening the gaits, producing some relaxed and expressive Medium level work in trot and canter. Then it was time to relax and walk on a long rein, and to reflect on what had been achieved. Sean said he felt that breathing out as a signal for downward transitions, and the shoulder-spin to aid engagement in canter, had both been very useful additions to his repertoire, and that they would be particularly helpful in future work with Harry.

While, on this occasion, Sean was working with a coach, it illustrates clearly how much can be achieved when there is a sense of shape and progress to the session. Because there is structure, it is easy to install this pattern into working on one's own, thus ensuring that every session results in progress at one level or another. Even if you find a session frustrating or difficult, you can still learn something that will be useful on another occasion – progress means shifts in your mind, and your horse's mind, just as much as 'improvement' in your observable performance together.

PART 5

Developing Magnificence

MAGNIFICENCE IS A BIG WORD, and as you read about the riders and horses I worked with to help in their solo schooling, I'd like you to be considering its implications, not only for them, but also for you and your horse. If your first reaction is that magnificence is rare, I'd like you to consider the proposition that it could be less rare – if only people were more able to realize the capabilities that are within them.

Coaching, as Gallwey discovered when he came to the conclusion that *Performance = Potential – Interference,* can help you discover your full potential by clearing your personal interference out of the way. And I'm arguing in this book that self-coaching can do the same. But magnificence is more than just realizing your potential. It's also being who you uniquely are, to the fullest of your capacity, whatever you may be doing – and knowing it.

Coaching is based on the assumption that each of us can be magnificent in our uniqueness, and that it's your coach's job to help you develop your self-belief so that you can own and express what is truly superb in yourself. Magnificence is not about achievement – although it may include it almost accidentally. In fact, there's potential magnificence in each and every one of us – when we are truly expressing who we are and realizing our capabilities.

How does coaching help this? Simply telling someone they're wonderful doesn't have this effect: for many people who lack confidence, praise can actually be a trigger that pushes an old 'if you really knew…' button. Even if they can accept praise, often the effect 'wears off'. But when you discover for yourself that you have a capability you hadn't previously realized, or resources to solve a problem you previously thought beyond you, then you know *from the inside* that you're worth something.

Coaching gets you to reach inside yourself. That's why the riders I worked with used phrases like 'makes me think', 'gets me into a discussion', 'helps me discover things about myself I didn't realize before' and 'spills over into the rest of my life'. Coaching *engages* you and, like your horse, when you're engaged your energy and capability are more fully at your disposal.

This supportively curious approach is one that's easily learnt. As mentioned earlier, the NLP word for learning by experience is 'modelling': someone else models how to do something in such a clear, detailed and explicit way that you are able to copy and make the behaviour and the attitudes your own. So, when people experience good coaching, they learn what's involved in being a coach, and can transfer the skill to coaching themselves. That's what this book has been about, and that was my intention in working with Nikki, Sean and Nicky. I wasn't *teaching* them, but offering them an experience of coaching which I knew they could internalize, and hoped they would use for themselves in their solo schooling.

Magnificence is what can result when people become self-actualizing, in the way that the psychologist Abraham Maslow described in the 1960s: knowing fully what is special about yourself and taking a quiet satisfaction and pride in it, so that you become radiantly at ease, whatever you're doing. The Renaissance thinkers called this quality *sprezzatura* – a condition of apparent effortlessness, even when effort is involved. It's the effortlessness of a great jumping round; of an expressive and fluent Kür where the music, the horse and the rider are inextricably one; of Mark Todd riding Badminton with one stirrup after the other had broken. It's also everyday riding events that you'd hardly think of describing to anyone else, yet you know you had a great ride.

For self-actualization brings with it the possibility of what Maslow called Peak Experiences – times when everything seems harmoniously and intensely focused and when you experience the elation of feeling at one with yourself and what you are doing. The *content* of a peak experience doesn't have to be unusual: it's the *process* that is special. Coaching, including self-coaching, helps you to become more 'present' in yourself and your experience, so it increases the likelihood that you will enjoy peak experiences in your riding. It helps you to become fully engaged – and this kind of moment-by-moment engagement involves awareness at many levels: your senses, your emotions, your intellect – any or all may be involved. You may have a peak experience on an ordinary hack or in a moment of quiet schooling. Although it may not give you a recognizable 'story' to tell someone else, you will have experienced it as intense, or in some way transforming. As one of my teachers used to say, 'I love it when things come together'.

In the brief accounts that follow, I'm going to describe the coaching alliances I developed with Nikki, Nicky and Sean and what we did in our sessions together. And I'm going to use their own words to express how this helped them engage in a new way with their own riding, so that they were able to coach themselves more effectively and express more fully their own magnificence and that of their horses.

Nikki G

Nikki and I have been friends for some years, and she was one of the case-study riders for *Schooling Problems Solved with NLP*. From the outset, she has been fascinated by NLP and found it very helpful in building her self-confidence as a rider and a teacher. In fact, she said that it was partly because of the work we did that she found enough self-belief to leave her non-horsy job and take up her interrupted career as a riding teacher. We developed an

'When things come together...' Nikki and Beamish.

informal pattern of swapping lessons with each other, and we have both found this enjoyable and helpful.

When I suggested that we might change the emphasis of our work from teaching to coaching, Nikki quickly agreed. She had two objectives for our work together: specifically, to receive a good assessment at the TTT (the classical riding trust which we both belong to) and, more broadly, to help her new horse, Beamish, learn to carry himself with greater fluency, freedom and grace.

When we began our coaching sessions together, I made a deliberate effort to stop 'teaching' Nikki and to engage her more by asking questions and getting her to pay attention to what was 'observable, interesting and relevant' in her experience and in the way Beamish was going. We certainly continued to address some old issues – notably Nikki's well-ingrained habit of collapsing in the waist and looking down – in close association with the new issues that Beamish brought with him: a longish back, heavy head and neck and a habit of leaning on his rider's hands. But we were also able to capitalize on Nikki's commitment and her enthusiastic engagement with the ideas and process of coaching, as well as Beamish's genuine nature, rhythmical gaits and lateral suppleness.

Beamish: a longish back, heavy head and neck and a habit of leaning on his rider's hands.

Nikki and Beamish – lighter in spirit as well as in the forehand.

We found in working together that play was our strongest ally, and that when we allowed ourselves to make the most of the momentary issues and opportunities that presented themselves in any session, we inevitably got something really useful out of it. Letting the situation tell us what was needed, and using a coaching approach to check how this related to Nikki's overall goals, as well as to the specific needs of the day, meant that we often worked on one or, at the most, two issues in any one session. This meant that we were able to be both relaxed and focused – setting a pattern which soon included Beamish, too, so that he became lighter in spirit as well as in the forehand. Less was, indeed, more.

Nikki received a glowing appraisal from her assessment at the TTT, and in the last sessions we had together before I sat down to write this, Beamish produced light and flexible transitions between a shortened, energetic trot and a bigger, longer trot. The peak moment of the sessions – for all three of us – was when he gave Nikki some powerful, expressive and balanced work, continuing to carry himself 'uphill' even when she gave him the rein to check his independence.

Nikki's Account

What do I feel I have achieved through Wendy's coaching sessions?

1. They have allowed me the freedom to experiment and 'play' during my riding.

2. They have given me access to NLP techniques which have made me aware of how I work and how to capitalize on my good points and improve or stretch myself in other areas.

3. They have taken the pressure away from schooling sessions, leaving me free to enjoy them rather than becoming stressed and worked-up about them.

4. My horse is more relaxed and is enjoying his work.

5. Rather than concentrating on getting things 'right' (making me 'tense' rather than 'toned'), I can now think more about patterns and schooling exercises to help engage the horse and get him thinking, rather than ploughing round and round the school getting more and more frustrated.

6. There are no 'rights and wrongs' and no 'black-and-white'. I can now use feedback that I am sensing or feeling in my own right, or that my horse is feeding back to me, in a constructive way in order to change or improve the way we are working together.

7. As a coach myself, these sessions have made me much more aware of how I talk to and train my pupils, and I now endeavour to coach in an NLP style where appropriate, rather than 'teaching' all the time.

If I had to use two words to describe what I have got from our sessions they would be:

'**Enabled**' and '**Empowered**'

About ten days after writing this, Nikki phoned to tell me about a brilliant schooling session she had just had with Beamish. 'It's amazing', she said, 'now I just can't wait to ride on my own – I'm impatient when other people are there. I just like to think it through myself.'

Nicky M

Nicky is a journalist, whom I first met when I did a reader phone-in for the horse magazine she worked for. When I arrived to do my session, she told me that she was embarrassed because, only a few days earlier, she had retired from a dressage competition I was judging when her mare, Lucinda, spooked after a few movements. I remembered the event – in fact, I'd been surprised because it was evident that both horse and rider had talent and I expected the horse to settle down, like a number of others who had spooked at the same things around the arena. In fact, I'd written 'Retired – what a pity!' on the sheet.

I decided to ask Nicky whether she would like us to work together on this as a case-study for the book, and was very pleased when she agreed. We decided that it would be a good idea to have some coaching sessions on the telephone in between our mounted work, as this would allow us to explore some of Nicky's thinking and feeling issues independently from her riding. In all, we had four mounted and three telephone sessions, the last of which was a couple of days before Nicky and Lucinda's Novice test in the Winter Semi-Finals.

We agreed that our most important aim was to help Nicky feel differently about any problems or mistakes in tests so that, in the split seconds that followed, she would be able to carry on instead of withdrawing. And the key here seemed to be helping Nicky to reframe performance as less of a 'success/failure' issue, and problems more as issues to work with rather than overwhelming disasters. Keeping focused on maintaining her communication with Lucinda, instead of worrying about how others would see their 'failure' to 'get it right', seemed to make a difference that went far beyond changing Nicky's behaviour and influenced her at the higher logical levels of belief, and even identity.

When it came to our mounted sessions, we found ourselves working to increase the freedom and trust between Nicky and Lucinda. Nicky's willingness to ride her sharp and active mare longer, looser and more forward, produced a greater harmony through the rein and much more softness and engagement from Lucinda. The contrast between the technically accurate but rather tight work of the first session and the expressive and generous harmony of the later sessions was lovely for Nicky to experience and for me to watch.

In particular, Nicky became much more generous to herself when things didn't go exactly to plan in tests, and she remained in the arena. This meant that, despite occasionally losing marks through 'mistakes', the partnership were still able to show their talent and get placed. The new Nicky was delighted

'...a much greater harmony through the rein and much more softness and engagement'.

with coming third, because it represented a real achievement at several levels. And when they got to the Winter Semi-Finals and Nicky left out one particular movement, she was able to transform her momentary flash of irritation, refocus on her conversation with Lucinda and come third again, qualifying for the Finals. I knew from the way she told me about it afterwards that, although it was still important to her to do well, she now had a much broader sense of what that meant: her complex equivalent for it had really changed.

Nicky's Account

What I've Achieved from NLP

Before I started my NLP sessions with Wendy, I knew I was heading somewhere I didn't want to go with my dressage. I knew that Lucinda and I were capable of doing well and even winning at Novice level, and I suppose that's what made it hard to accept the days when things went wrong. My expectations of us were increasing and, as a result, our performance was beginning to deteriorate. I was more tense at competitions and in schooling sessions (because I wanted perfection and didn't want other people to see that I had failed) and on bad days, I would frequently retire from tests and then be miserable for the rest of the day – or even week, sometimes.

Despite people suggesting I could change, I was adamant that it was my personality and that, when I became this frustrated person, I was no longer in control of my actions, thoughts, feelings, etc. I did want to change but I didn't know how to go about it.

NLP was, in the first instance, a good reason for me to try to change. Although a little sceptical and unsure of what NLP coaching could do for me, I think I went in with a positive attitude and tried my best to make it work. I can't really put my finger on what work we did in the school, or any particular telephone conversation I had with Wendy that played a big part in my change of character, but I started to look at things in a different way.

Here are some of the thoughts I used to help me put things into perspective:

1. My horse costs me £450 a month. If I am not enjoying the time I spend riding her then there really is no point in having her. (This always had a positive effect, because I don't want to sell her and can't imagine life without horses.)

2. Who really cares whether I win or lose a competition? I know people are pleased if their friends and family do well, but ultimately everyone leads a

busy lifestyle and they are too wrapped up in what they are doing to ponder much on my performances. I thought about my reactions when my friends do well or badly at shows. I am pleased or disappointed for them, but I never judge them if they do badly – or even give it a second thought really – which is what I thought other people were doing about me.

3. The majority of judges want you to do well. They are not sitting in their car at C thinking 'I hope this person does a terrible test!'

4. In the great scheme of things, how much does it matter if things go wrong? Now, when they do, I ask myself: 'Did I enjoy that test? What went wrong and how can I improve next time? What do I need to work on in our schooling sessions between now the and next outing to increase our marks?'

I have been out to four or five shows since starting the sessions, and although some of the tests have not gone as well as they might, I have thankfully remained calm – reminding myself of the points previously mentioned.

One of the biggest things I have noticed is that I apply this change of philosophy to everyday life – without realizing it much of the time – and I've noticed that this has a number of positive effects, such as forestalling arguments which were about to happen, getting what I wanted out of a situation rather than keeping quiet and getting nowhere, and having a positive effect on other people who are being negative. I have had days when the old feelings of losing focus on reality started to arise and, so far, I have managed to make them go away again by changing my thought processes very quickly.

As an example, Lucinda had a day recently when she wasn't in the mood for schooling (it was very wet and windy), but I felt I had to ride her as we had a competition coming up. She was totally uncooperative and spooky and my riding started to get worse (I began to use more rein contact, became more tense and I could feel frustration rising). I changed my thought processes, but the horrible side kept taking priority. I just couldn't beat it using my thoughts. In the end I decided to return to walk until I was calm, think about something else for a while, and then work on something Lucinda found more fun –and it worked!

In summary, this is what I feel I have got out of the sessions:

• A different perspective of what really matters in life.

• A better relationship and more trust with my horse, friends and family.

• I'm a happier person for other people and my horse to be around.

• There is more focus on preparatory work for competition.

• There is an increase in positive thought processes such as 'How can I resolve this? What do I want to achieve?'

A couple of weeks after supplying this account, Nicky sent me an e-mail, adding an unexpected coda:

> Something struck me yesterday. A girl in the office asked me whether I thought NLP had played a big part in my qualifying for the Winter Champs. I said yes definitely, without hesitation, and she asked me why. I explained how much calmer I was in tests and how the test I rode at Hurstbourne wasn't a great one and before I would have become worked up. Anyway, it suddenly dawned on me that not only would I have become worked up, but I would have retired! I can't remember the last time I went wrong in a test and carried on. So you could say NLP is the reason why we qualified.

Getting it all together. Nicky and Lucinda at the Winter Finals.

Sean

Sean is a professional rider, who still trains and rides event horses, although nowadays he also does pure dressage. When we started our work together, it seemed to me that the way he rode communicated a degree of diffidence about doing dressage which really didn't match up with his subtle feel for his horses and his ability to get them working freely forward.

I had known Sean slightly for some years before we started working together, seeing him at competitions and occasionally judging him. From the outset, I thought he was very talented but that he somehow looked rather apologetic about his riding. One of his horses who had particularly impressed me was Georgie Boy, then working at Novice level. Georgie is half Clydesdale – a huge and rather unlikely dressage horse – but I really liked Georgie's big, rhythmical stride, and was impressed by his softness, elasticity and balance.

At one competition I overheard Sean saying that he needed to 'get his head

Sean looking 'rather apologetic' with Kluedo.

around lateral work' now that Georgie was moving up the levels, and this phrasing told me that Sean might be interested in using NLP to achieve what he wanted. By the time we actually managed to coordinate our diaries I was starting work on this book, and I suggested that we might take a coaching approach to our sessions.

My agenda for our sessions was to help Sean grow into a stronger sense of his considerable ability as a dressage rider. I thought that, although he was already very effective, he could project more presence in the arena – and become even more effective in communicating with his horses – by adopting more of a classical position. Although we had originally planned to work just with Georgie, he wasn't available for every one of our seven coaching sessions, so we ended up having three with Georgie, two with Kluedo and one with Harry.

This variety meant that, as well as working with Sean, we were dealing with his separate agendas for the three different horses. While I was dipping into my technical knowledge, I was offering it in an experimental way rather than as 'teaching'. The test of any strategy I proposed for helping each horse to develop in freedom and lightness – and in the lateral work which had been our starting point – was whether Sean found it useful and, if so, how. While a coach may know where it's useful to direct attention, only the person being coached can make that information their own and evaluate its usefulness to *them*.

In thinking about our coaching, Sean picked on one particular example of how it differed from being taught: he remembered that I had followed up one particular suggestion (which he carried out) by asking him *how he had gone about doing what I asked*. Asking him *how* he did it required him to go inside himself to find out (it was a search question) – and when he found out, he knew something extra about his own processing, and so gained something over and beyond the technical tip itself. I think this is a really important example and I was delighted that, when he thought about our sessions later, it was this kind of process that Sean remembered as distinctive of the work we'd done together. This illustrates a key way in which coaching differs from instruction. Because the person being coached is required to find out what it takes within their own mind and body to make a strategy happen, or to try it out and evaluate its usefulness as against other possibilities, they interact with it rather than receiving it passively. And, because of this, new information that's first incorporated at the level of **conscious incompetence** (*'I didn't know that before'*) can be practised until it becomes initially part of **conscious competence** (*'I can do this now'*) and finally an unquestioned, automatic part of **unconscious competence**. (A fuller account of this sequence is given in the first chapter of *Schooling Problems Solved with NLP*.)

Like the other riders in the case-studies, Sean had had good teaching, in his case from established – even prestigious – trainers. As his comments show, although he enjoyed and valued this traditional instruction, he felt he gained something different from being coached: a reinforcement of his independent ability to direct his learning and train his horses. Coaching helped him to feel more confident in his skills: even his more upright posture grew from the inside out as, a true symbol and example of his increased authority and presence. Georgie and Kluedo both qualified for the Winter Semi-Finals at Medium level. On the day, Georgie was so much in performance mode that he did piaffe while waiting to enter the arena – and went from a floating excitement to exhaustion as the test progressed! Nonetheless, he achieved a respectable score and placing. And Kluedo went on to qualify for the National Finals.

Sean's Account

Being coached is like having a conversation, having a discussion. If I go to a trainer for a lesson and I do as he asks I can feel really pleased that I've made an improvement. But, somehow, since I've been working with you the horses have been going better and winning more. It's like I'm more involved because we've been having a discussion.

When you're having a lesson you're told what to do. You may be too shy to ask how to do something, or to say you haven't understood. It's a confidence thing – to say 'Does that mean I should be doing that with my leg, or this with my arm?' But when you're having a discussion your personal input is as important, or even more important.

When you said to me about stabilizing my right hand by having my right elbow on my hip – and then asked what process I used in order to do that – you broke it down into a small chunk, and that made a huge amount of difference. I realized how my contact had previously been contributing to the horse's lack of straightness, and how immediately straightness had improved when I anchored the contact in the way you suggested. And on the video of Georgie at the Winter Semis you can see that my right hand is absolutely still and so he's quite straight.

Trainers are usually looking for the big picture. Everybody wants to be a winner – the person having the lesson wants value for money and the trainer knows that. This means they tend to feel it's not enough to spend time on small detail like this. They're missing the point that focusing on something small can have a bigger effect. I've been to bigger and better trainers and not got that little key thing out of it – that little bit, the missing link.

Even when I know a trainer well personally, when I go for a formal lesson he puts his professional hat on and I put my schooling hat on – there's a definite shift. I knew I rode crookedly, but even though I'd be working on that at home I wasn't going to want to tell him about it. It's a question of confidence. My trainer could yell at me to sit more upright or get my bloody shoulders back… but when a friend saw me riding at the Semi-Finals after our coaching work together he said 'I've never seen you ride so upright'.

When you go to a trainer they're not necessarily going to use your language, your metaphors, so if you're any good you're going to translate in order to get the most out of them. Coaching is about finding out how the person processes information and using it to teach them.

It's having the confidence to go home and play – not being afraid to make mistakes, because it's from this that you may learn something. Through little things we've worked on together, I've kept on top of riding by myself. I've taken them on board and regularly kept reminding myself of them until they became automatic. I've got more to refer to when things begin to fall apart. That's because the work we've done, we've done together, so I understood the 'hows' and 'whys'. With coaching, you understand it more because you've had a conversation about it. It's a more personal thing. You couldn't go around

I had just asked Sean to stabilize his elbows by tucking them into the hollow above his hip bones. As his account in the text records, this 'small' alteration produced huge results.

'I've never seen you ride so upright.' Sean and Kluedo at the Winter Finals.

universally saying this is what you do in a particular situation, like a rule of thumb. It's a much more individual thing, a 50/50 experience with your coach. So you end up with more armour that fits you to use on your own.

Marisian – the Ultimate Solo Schooler

Marisian is a family friend we've known for a number of years. Now in her mid-twenties, she's had her own ponies and ridden since she was a child. She showjumped successfully in national competitions, and even then enjoyed schooling her own and other people's ponies almost more than competing herself.

Pre-university, she spent nearly a year working for a well-known dressage rider and trainer, with whom she honed her highly developed natural observation skills, as well as her ability to get horses working freely forward with engagement and balance.

Having acquired a number of ponies and begun breeding and bringing on youngsters, Marisian chose to take an Open University degree, which allowed her to keep her riding and schooling going while she studied, and she was later able to maintain this alongside developing her career in management consultancy. Like many solo schoolers, she has a very busy life! She competes only rarely – although when she does, her 13.2hh pony, Prudie, more than holds her own in dressage against horses. After one competition an international trainer was so impressed with their performance that he followed her out to the lorry-park and offered to train her, on her pony.

I knew from the outset of planning this book that I wanted to write something about Marisian, because she manages to build great rapport with her youngsters and helps them develop with freedom and fluency, although she works on her own, with almost no formal instruction. She has trained in NLP – but actually her training only confirmed communication skills which she already had, and which she was using very successfully.

What Marisian enjoys most is building the kind of conversations with her horses that I've been talking about in my books: ones which involve mutual attention and respect, discovering and developing the innate abilities of each pony so that he can be the best that he can be. As she works alone, long-reining and lungeing as often as actually riding, these are some of the things she's aiming for.

Marisian's Aims and Reflections

- I want a horse who feels right. I can see this from the ground, and I can feel them softening in my fingers when I lunge them.

- When I was a kid, I used to spend hours playing with those long ribbons you use for making gymnastic patterns: in my mind that's how a horse should be going – with fluency and suppleness and freedom, just flowing from one movement into another without a break.

- I want them going forward and to be using their muscles. I want them to be in front of my leg, accurate, and listening – not just reacting.

- I like to work for what they've got, not what they haven't.

- Their personality and my mood have to be taken into account. If I'm not in the right mood, I get off.

An afternoon's schooling session with Marisian and Prudie. (a) Stretch and warm-up.

(b) Working out.

(c) Playing with shoulder-in to increase engagement.

(d) Becoming more 'uphill'.

(e) Cooling down. 'Enough...'

- I love watching ponies who I've trained with a child on board – that way, you know you haven't cut corners.

- When I'm riding I'm in-time. My breathing goes differently. It's about unconscious competence – in-time and in the moment.

How does she coach herself? Rather than analysing how she goes about it, I'm going to let Marisian's own words speak for her. They demonstrate perfectly, without any additional comment, how solo schooling can be a process of self-realization and self-development that the rider engages in both mounted and dismounted, involving mind and body and every level of functioning. And it is through the rider's commitment to the process that both rider and horse are enabled to become, in each other's company, the best that they can be.

- You need to keep assessing yourself – I spend more time reflecting than riding.

- I'm always looking to find which way of communicating is right for them.

- I replay in my mind how someone rides. I ask myself 'How did they get the horse to do that – what would have to be happening for me to hold myself like that?'

- When I have a bad ride I think about it.

- I think about how my body impacts on the horse.

- I might spend three hours thinking about a particular horse before I can go to sleep.

- It's like having a language in your head about different horses – how they need to move. It's all about how they *could* be.

- It's about having enough confidence in myself and the horse.

Marisian with Feargus. (a) Warming up – forward and energetic.

(b) Proceeding in balance and self-carriage – working collected.

(c) Cooling down – stretching into a longer frame.

Marisian with Jezebel. (a) Jezebel hadn't worked for nearly a year, so Marisian began with lungeing.

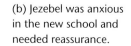

(b) Jezebel was anxious in the new school and needed reassurance.

(c) After twenty minutes she was confident and going forwards calmly on a loose rein.

Marisian and Charlie. From an energetic stretch *(above)* to forward, balanced roundness, all on a light contact *(below)*.

Conclusion

IT'S THESE QUALITIES OF UNIQUENESS, harmony, authenticity and self-belief that a coach is seeking to promote in anyone they work with, regardless of the specific goals they are working towards. Often, this is the most important thing a coach does, because it's from this basis, far more than from acquiring specific knowledge or learning particular skills, that people are able to solve their problems and achieve what they want. And that's why it's proper to call coaching an alliance rather than a teaching or helping relationship – because both parties put themselves into their work together and both gain something from it. There is a great joy in helping someone to realize their magnificence.

It's been my experience that, when you're coached, you learn how to self-coach: the process transfers in the most natural way to become your property. This was my aim in working with the riders who generously agreed to help me with my case-studies, and it's my hope that, in the process of reading this book, you too will have begun to engage in that process and make it your own.

I like to remember Charles de Kunffy's words:

Provided he understands his horses well, the rider will have created beauty that is the physical aesthetic manifestation of his intellectual understanding and spiritual depth. So can man be elevated by the taming of his horse, through a partnership with him, to become himself the object and subject of his art.

Charles de Kunffy *The Ethics and Passions of Dressage*

I hope that, by now, you will have started to believe that you, as well as your horse, have your own magnificence. I also hope that, as a result of reading this book, you'll have discovered some strategies for becoming your own generous, supportive yet truthful coach. And I believe that, as you ride your horse as well and as sympathetically as you can, and coach yourself with curiosity about what is observable, interesting and relevant, you will be engaging in a process that releases magnificence in both of you.

APPENDIX

Sub-modalities

When we think, we use our senses, especially the visual, auditory and kinesthetic, for internal processing. These are our **representational systems** or **sensory modalities**. Within each system, different sub-sets of information may be being called upon, and each one of us will tend to respond more to some of these than to others. NLP calls these **sub-modalities**. For example, whereas a 'visual' person is more influenced by colour, finding bright colours more attractive (or more frightening) than pale ones – whether they are looking at something external or imagining/recalling it internally – someone else who is more 'auditory' may be influenced by the *tone* of what they're hearing, or replaying in their heads, more than by its *volume*. We are all different.

If you want to use your representational systems more effectively to enhance something you are imagining or, alternatively, to know how to change or 'play down' the effect of something which alarms or limits you, you'll find it really helpful to ascertain which sub-modalities are particularly influential for you. Here are some of the distinctions that can be made within the three most influential representational systems:

Visual

Brightness	Contrast	Flat/3D
Size	Clarity	Associated/dissociated
Colour/black-and-white	Movie/still	Frame/panorama

Auditory

Pitch	Rhythm	Volume
Tonality	Distance	Clarity
Resonance		

Kinesthetic

Pressure	Location	Texture
Temperature	Movement	Duration
Intensity	Shape	

Working with Sub-modalities

- Take one of your strongly positive representations and notice which aspects are key for you.

- Take a negative representation and do the same (work with a mild example at first).

- Are the same sub-modalities at work in the two, or are they different?

- Return to your positive representation, and investigate what happens if you change your key sub-modality (for example, by increasing black-and-white contrast, softening colour brilliance, raising pitch, decreasing pressure, etc.).

- What effect does this have on the representation – does it make it less or more attractive? The object is to experiment and find out how you can influence your own representations so that they are more effective and less hindering.

- If the change made your representation less effective/attractive, you now have confirmation that this variable is a key one for you – and you can put things back how they were. Increase the brilliance again; turn up the volume, or whatever.

- If your change made the representation more attractive/useful, keep the change. Now take other representations you have and discover what happens if you make a similar change there. Better again? Great!

- Now take your mildly unpleasant representation, find the key sub-modality (ies) and experiment the other way about. If it's in colour, what happens if you make it paler, or black-and-white? What happens if you make it still rather than moving? What happens if you lower the pitch, make the sound come from further away, add white noise or cheerful music to interfere with it? If it's hot, what happens if you make it cooler? If heavy, try making it lighter... and so on.

• Carry on experimenting until you find what's most effective – and until you build a good personal profile of what's key for you. Then you can use this information to enhance or modify other experiences or thoughts as they come along.

Taking Things Further

If you would like some NLP coaching to help you develop your riding skills, you can contact me by telephone on (UK code) 01273-492848, or via my e-mail:

wendyandleo.jago@virgin.net

Bear in mind that off-horse coaching can often help you to formulate and achieve your riding goals, or unlock persistent problems, just as much as – sometimes more than – mounted lessons. There is a place for both.

The following is a list of further reading on subjects related to this book:

NLP and Riding

Jago, Wendy, *Schooling Problems Solved with NLP*, J. A. Allen (London) 2001.

Coaching

Flaherty, James, *Coaching: Evoking Excellence in Others*, Butterworth Heinemann (Boston) 1999.

Gallwey, Timothy, *The Inner Game* series of books on golf, tennis, skiing, etc. (Pan Books (London) 1986.

— *Work*, Random House (New York) 2000.

(Even though Gallwey's books are concerned with activities other than riding, they are immensely readable and take you through the principles of coaching that Gallwey discovered and formulated.)

Leonard, Thomas J., *The Portable Coach,* Scribner (New York) 1998.

McDermott, Ian and Jago, Wendy, *The NLP Coach,* Piatkus (London) 2001.

NLP

McDermott, Ian and Shircore, Ian, *Manage Yourself, Manage Your Life,* Piatkus (London) 1999.

O'Connor, Joseph and McDermott, Ian, *Principles of NLP,* Thorsons (London) 1996.

Index

Note: Page numbers in **bold** refer to figures or photographs

The names of horses and of works are given in *italics*

accepting yourself 17–18
aids
    canter transitions 8, 108–9
    strength of 36–8
    weight 153–5
Amanda 82
'amateur' rider 111–12
'and' 137
anger 128–9
anticipation, horse's 43–4
'apart from' 133
approach, methods *see* method of approach
'as' 138
'as-if' frame 116–23
assumptions 11–12, 23
attention, of rider 21–2
auditory senses 219
away from motivation
    horse 100–2
    rider 71–4

Beamish **22**, 60–4, 122–3, **130**, 140–2, 174, 196–8
behavioural traps 160–2
belief, problems of 162–6
beliefs and values 56–7, 63
Bella 70
Billy 103
blame-frame 22
body-mind connection 13, 129–31, 139–40
books, reading 45

breathing, rider's **119**, 172–4, 189
'but' 133

calibration 18, 45–7
    skill-building tips 48–9
'can't' 134–5
canter
    improving engagement 190–1
    transitions 8, 43–4, 108–9
capability 62–3, 159–60
Carrie 81
Cathy 85
celebration 185–6
centre of gravity, rider's 174
change, calibration 18, 45–9
Charlie **47**, **134**, **215**
Charlotte 147
children 16, 167
choices 14–15
chunk size preference
    horse 98–100, 108–9
    rider 67–70
chunking 60–4, 108–9, 146, 152–5, 157
Clara 77–8
classical riding 149
coach 6–7
coaching
    compared with teaching 6, 170, 205–8
    development 7
    feedback 163–4
    potential of 194
    and self-coaching 216
coaching approach 144–5
coaching questions 176–9
cobs 159–60
communication
    effective 25–6

with horse 25, 179–80
key abilities 18–19
compelling future 47, **48**
competition 147–8
framing/reframing 113–14, 199–203
complex equivalents 111–12, 135
cool-down 191–2, **211**, **213**
coordination 7–8
creativity 149–50, 153
Critic 149, 150
curiosity 176
curiosity frame 22, 30, 112–13, 116, 141

de Kunffy, Charles 41, 47, 90, 114, 164–5, 190, 216
difference that makes the difference 51, 52–3
differences, calibrating 18, 45–9
Dilts, Robert 146, 149, 153
directional motivation
horse 100–2
rider 71–4
Disney, Walt 149
downward transitions 52–3, 55–6
Drammie (The Dramatist) 120–2
Dreamer 146, 149–50
dressage
framing 29–30
procedural approach 91–2
dressage test
chunking down 153
words for 132

elbows, stabilizing 206, **207**
emotions, human 13, 27–8, 43, 128–9
engagement 169–70, **171**
improving 157, 190–1, **210**
Ethics and Passions of Dressage, The 216
eventers, and dressage 29–30
experience, levels of 56–8
experimenting 172–4
exploration 184
external referenced *see* other-referenced
eyes closed, riding with 48–9

failure, and identity 57–8
fear 33, 53–4
Feargus **48**, **213**
feedback 163–4
filtering 165
from curiosity and questions 35–6
'feel' 41
feet, position in stirrups 53
first position 19

flow 45
fluency 183–4
flying changes 108–9
focus
relaxed 9, 19–20
of work session 181, 185
forward thinking 186–7
fowardness, lack of 51
frame of reference *see* source of reference
framing 29–30, 109, 110–12
'as-if' frame 116–19
curiosity frame 22, 30, 112–13, 116, 141
success/failure 8–9, 113–15, 199–203
of work session 184
work sessions using 120–3
Frankie 70

Gallwey, Timothy 7–8, 16, 20, 30, 35–6, 44, 140, 166, 186
Georgie Boy **11**, 98–9, 107–9, **171**, 204–5, 206
goals 13–14, 144–7
chunking up and down 146, 152–7
NLP criteria 151–2
recognising 'real' 147–8
'thinking outside the box' 146, 149–50
work sessions using 156–7
Grace 78

hacking 33, 53–4
half-halt 52–3, 172–3
half-pass 69–70
halt 176–7
hands of rider 35
Harry **29**, 187–92
Henry 86
here-and-now 19–20, **21**, 161
hollow back, horse's 52
honesty 147–8
horse
anticipation 43–4
communication with 25, 179–80
and human emotions 13, 27–8, 43, 128–9
metaprogrammes 95–106
states 27, 167
horse profiles
chunk size preference 98–9
direction of motivation 100–1
method of approach 102–4
source of reference 104–5
horse-rider match 106
'how' questions 178
human emotions 128–9

identity 56, 57–8, 63
imagery 129–31
in-the-moment 161
in-time orientation 82–6
information, filtering 31–2
interference, sources of 7–9
internal dialogues
    language used 131–2
    self-critical 25–6, 148, 163–4
internal reference see self-reference
internal scenarios 117–18

'jack-of-all-trades' 77, 110–11
Jezebel **214**
Jo 120–2
Josie 81
judgements
    calibration as 49
    success/failure 8–9, 113–15
'just' 133

Karen 103
killer weasels 133–6
kinesthetic reframe 111
kinesthetic representational system 28–9,
41, 219
Kleudo **145**, 156–7, **173**, **204**, **208**
Kottas, Arthur 46, 108–9

language 110–11, 124–5, 207
    changing use of 131–2
    and chunk size preference 68
    and directional motivation 72
    importance for riding 124–5
    and method of approach 75
    mind-body connection 129–31, 139–40
    and orientation in time 83
    for riding experience 125–7
    and source of reference 79–80
    and states 127–9
    work sessions 139–42
    see also words
'lazy' 135
leading questions 176–9
learning
    marking 186
    in play state 16–17, 169
leg position 32–3, 53, 61–4
lengthened strides 160
Leo 18, 147
'less is more' 36–8
limitations 159–60, 163–4
Lizzie 69–70
logical levels 56–8

Lolly **27**, 101, **119**, 139–40, 153–4, 172–3,
    187
Lucinda **8**, **21**, 90–4, 114, **171**, 199–203
Lucy 74

magnificence 194, 195
    realization of 216–17
Marisian **36**, **47–8**, **112**, 118, **134**, **169**,
    213–15
    aims and reflections 209, 212
    background 208–9
Maslow, Abraham 15, 195
Merlin 104
meta-programmes 31–2, 65–6
    chunk size preference 67–70
    directional motivation 71–5
    horse 95–106
    method of approach 75–8
    orientation in time 82–6
    plotting profiles 86–9
    source of reference 78–82
    work sessions 90–4, 107–9
metaphors 127, 129–30, 207
method of approach
    horse 102–4
    rider 74–8
Mike 77–8
mind-body connection 13, 129–31, 139–40
mismatching 167
modelling 32–3, 178
monitoring, self 18–19
motivation tips
    chunk size preference 68
    and direction of motivation 72
    and method of approach 76
    orientation in time 84
    source of reference 80
motivational direction
    horse 100–2
    rider 71–4
muscle tension 20

Neuro-Linguistic Programming (NLP)
    coaching approach 9–11
    goals 151–2
Nicky M **8**, **21**, 132, 145, **171**
    metaprogrammes 90–4
    own account of work sessions 201–3
    success/failure frame 114, 199–201
    summary of work sessions 199–201
Nikki G **22**, 35, 122–3, 145
    changing state 167
    devloping magnificence 195–8
    own account of work sessions 198–9

posture 130–1, 140–1, **142**, 174
summary of work sessions 195–8
triangulation 51, 59–64
NLP *see* Neuro-Linguistic Programming

observation 40
calibration 45–6
criteria for items 44–5
of self 18–19
see also sensory acuity
on the bit 52
'only' 134
optimist 66
options approach
horse 102–3
rider 74–7
orientation in time 82–6, 91
other-referenced
horse 104–5
rider 79–82
'ought' 45, 148
outcomes
well-formed 13–14
see also goals
owning your riding 146–7, 155–6

pacing 97–8
patterns 43–4, 49
peak experiences 195
perceptual positions 18–19, 42–5, 54, 149
'perching', in saddle 30, 120–2
perfectionism 164–6, 199–203
performance, components 7–8
pessimist 66
pirouette, walk 98–9, 107–8
play state 167–74, 198
action 169–70
and learning 16–17, 169
permission 16–17, 168
pleasure 168–9
work sessions using 172–4
'yes' attitude 170–1
playing safe 160–1
ponies **134**, 159–60
position of rider
and horse's engagement 190–1
metaphors 129–31
modelling 32–3
reframing of problems 30, 120–2
use of triangulation 60–4
practice
internal 117–18
negative effects 161–2, 184
praise 8–9, 194

pressure 20
presuppositions 12, 23–4
enabling 24–5
hidden 24
procedures approach
horse 102–4
rider 75–8, 91–2
'professional' rider 111–12
Prudie **36**, **112**, **169**, **210–11**

questions
feedback from 35–6
horse 179–80
leading 176–9

Rachel 74
reading books 45
Realist 151
reflection 186–7
reframing 30, 110–12, 120–2, 200–3
rehearsals, internal 117–18
relaxed focus 9, 19–20
reliance on others 162–3
repetition 16–17, 161–2, 184
representational systems 28–9, 41, 55
and language 126–7
sub-modalities 55, 218–20
representations 117–18
resourcefulness
achieving 13, 120
assumptions of 11–12
resources 185
responsbility, taking 17–18
rhythm 48–9
rider profiles
chunk size preference 69–70
directional motivation 73–4
method of approach 77–8
orientation in time 85–6
sources of reference 81–2
rider-horse match 106
rigour 20–1
Rosewood 100–1

safety zone 160–1
Sally 85
Sam 70
Sandy 85–6
Schooling Problems Solved with NLP 114
schooling session see work session
Sean **11**, **29**, 145, **171**, **173**
and *Georgie Boy* 98–9, 107–9
goals 156–7
own account of work sessions 206–8

structuring work session 187–92
summary of work sessions 204–6
search question 35–6
searching 177–8
seat, deepening 127–8
second position 19, 42–3
Self One 7–8
Self Two 8
self-acceptance 17–18
self-actualization 194, 195
self-belief 194
self-carriage, horse 52, 157, 190–1, **213**
self-coaching 212, 216
self-criticism 163–4
self-reference
    horse 104–5
    rider 79
sensory acuity 18, 41, 48–9
sensory modalities *see* representational
systems
sensory system check 54, 55–6
serpentines 154–5
Shazam 73, 77
shoulder-in **210**
shoulder-spin, rider 190
singing 167
source of reference
    horse 104–5
    rider 78–82
Spock, Mr 153
sprezzatura 195
Star Trek 153
states 26–8, 166–7
    breaking 166–7
    horse's 27, 167
    and language 127–9
    play 16–17, 167–74, 198
    resourcefulness 13, 120
    trying 8, 30, 141, 166, 174
Steve 85–6
stiffness, horse 17
stirrups, position of feet 53
straightness 206, **207**
strategies, comparing effectiveness 53–4
stretch zone 15–16, 92
stretching tips
    chunk size preference 68–9
    directional motivation 72–3
    and method of approach 76–7
    orientation in time 84
    source of reference 80–1
sub-modalities 55, 218–20
success/failure frame 8–9, 113–15, 199–200
    indicators 115

reframing 200–3
Susie 73, 77, 110–11

teacher
    observational skills 40, 45–6
    reliance on 162–3
teaching, compared with coaching 6, 170,
    205–8
Ted 81
telephone coaching 199
thinking 28
third position 19
'though' 133
through-time perspective 83, 91
'throughness' 111, **112**
time, orientation in 82–6, 91
Tom 73
Tools for Dreamers 149
towards motivation
    horse 100–1
    rider 71–3
tracker weasels 136–9
transitions
    canter 8, 43–4, 108–9
    downward 52–3, 55–6
traps 158–9
    behavioural 160–2
    belief problems 162–6
    capability 159–60
'tree' metaphor 129–30
triangulation 50–1, 58–9
    how it works 52–4
    logical levels check 56–8
    sensory system check 55–6
    in work sessions 59–65
Tristan 102–3, 159
'try' 127, 133
'trying' state 8, 30, 141, 166, 174
tuning-in 183

unconscious processing 36

Vals 99, 104–5
values 56–7, 63
video, internal 33
visual calibration 18, 47
visual senses 218–20

waist, collapsing 174
walk pirouette 98–9, 107–8
warm-up 183–4, 187–9, **210**, **213**
weasel words 132
    killer 133–6
    tracker 136–9

weight aids 153–5
Wendy **27**, **119**
  breathing experiment 172–3
  chunking 153–5
  effect of words 139–40
  riding goals 147–8
'what if?'
  negative 136
  positive 137–8
'what?' questions 178–9
'while' 138
Wilde, Oscar 168
'wonder' 137
words
  success/failure frame 115
  weasel 133–9
  see also language

work session
  cool-down 185–7, 191–2
  focus of 181
  marking the learning 186
  thinking forward 186–7
  warm-up 183–4, 187–9
  when to stop 184
  workout 184–5, 189–91, **210**
workout 184–5, 189–91, **210**

'yes' attitude 170–1
'yet' 136–7

zones
  safety 160–1
  stretch 15–16, 92